Judging My Life

From Rags to Robes

Judging My Life

From Rags to Robes

An Autobiography

By Judge David Rosenberg

BookMasters, Inc.

Interior design by Aaron Wedra

Library of Congress control number: 2021942766

Published by BookMasters Inc.
ISBN: 978-0-692-03740-9

Dedicated to all those first generation kids from Poland, Ireland, China, Germany, Nigeria, Mexico, Italy, Honduras, India, Japan, France, Great Britain, Brazil, Pakistan, Lebanon, Australia, Ukraine, Greece, Algeria, Sudan, Iraq, Vietnam, Mali, South Korea, Afghanistan, Russia, and a hundred other nations and regions who came to the shores of the United States and aspired to dream the American dream.

Judging My Life

From Rags to Robes

Preface

Autobiographies are an interesting literary form. You can't write them at the beginning of your life because nothing has really been accomplished at that point in time, and if you speculate on what you might do in your life the work becomes one of fiction. So, generally, you write these autobiographies at a time in your life when you have something to say – if not in quality, then at least in quantity.

I wrote my autobiography primarily out of boredom. I started writing it when the COVID-19 pandemic hit in the middle of March 2020. At that point in time, most everything shut down and we were sheltering in place. For me, that meant months and months at home. The combination of factors (I am in my 70's, I was bored, I had little to do during the early stages of the pandemic, and I like to write) made this autobiography an inevitability. The deciding point occurred when I was asked to write a short article for "The Bench" (the magazine of the California Judiciary) – several Judges who were children of immigrants were asked to pen brief articles about their experiences. That brief article grew into this work.

As I reflected on my years, I realized two themes wound and rewound in my life's travels like strands of DNA.

First, I realized that at various stages of my life I had made what I will call "resolutions" to do certain things. Some of these resolutions were conscious, hard and fast. Others were quite sub-conscious, only being fully realized well after the fact. An example of my "resolutions" include the time I attended high school in Munich, Germany, evincing a strong desire to become a commissioned officer in the US Army and seeing that as a high calling. Another example occurred when I attended law school in Davis, California, being drawn to the political realm and desiring to work at the very top of the food chain for a Governor. These resolutions have driven my life's path.

Second, I realized that my life was a series of steps on a staircase, with one step leading inexorably to the next. My path seems to have been clearly marked and destined for me. For example, deciding to go to California at the age of 17 to attend college foretold my future.

Finally, I must pass along a little advice to future writers of books (including autobiographies). Many writers write the title first and then attempt to write the book. I think that's backwards. I recommend that you write the book, and then when you are done (or almost done) you write the title. The dog should wag the tail, not the other way around. And in the case of the title to this autobiography – I would not have thought of it at the beginning of my written journey. But it became quite obvious at the end.

One

Poland

Poor Poland. Poland has the historical misfortune to find itself wedged between the German Eagle to the West and the Russian Bear to the East, essentially between a rock and a hard place. And – when Poles are not fighting other Poles – the history of Poland is filled with a litany of invasion after invasion by one foreign regime after another.

Poland first became a recognized entity around the year 1000. In fact, at year 966, Mieszko the First was baptized and he adopted Catholicism as the nation's first official religion. Over the next century, most of the population of Poland converted to the Catholic faith.

The early history of Poland is replete with internal battles as one family or another took control of the emerging nation. Poland and Lithuania combined for a time to become a very powerful force in Europe. Then in the year 1241 the Mongols of the Golden Hoard invaded Poland from the south. In the middle of the 17th century a major Swedish invasion flowed in from the north. Poland under King Jan Sobieski saved Christianity in Europe when it repulsed the Ottoman Turks in 1683 at the gates of Vienna. There were numerous wars over the years against Russia. There was even a time around 1772 to 1795 that Poland essentially was dissolved as a state and was gobbled up by its neighbors. A piece of it went to Russia, a piece of it went to Prussia and a piece of it went to Austria. Napoleon Bonaparte, of all people, when he moved eastward into Russia recreated the Polish state. He called it the Duchy of Warsaw. So for another brief time the Polish state re-entered, albeit with a different name.

After the Napoleonic wars ended, however, Poland was again divided by the victors of the moment. In WWI the allies (of that time) agreed to restore Poland. And so the Polish state re-emerged. But that was short-lived. In 1939, at the very start of WWII, Poland was invaded by Germany in what was called the Blitzkrieg – a lightening-fast invasion of massive fire-power. A few weeks after the German invasion from the west, the Russians invaded Poland from the east. And so Poland was once again essentially dissolved throughout WWII. In 1945, after the war ended, Poland once again became an entity, however, only as a Russian puppet state. In the collapse of the Soviet Union, Poland has – once again – re-emerged as one of the most liberal democracies in Europe, and in fact is now a major part of the European Union.

Poland took quite a beating in WWII. It is estimated that at least 6 million Poles were killed in that war, and at least half of those were Polish Jews. A terrible toll of lost lives, families torn asunder, and fortunes dissipated.

Historically, Poland was one of the most tolerant countries in Europe for Jews. During the years 1000-1500 (a long stretch of time, 500 years, half of a millennium) a considerable number of Jews settled in Poland because it was a relatively tolerant place. Jews were the "pariah class" in the vast bulk of Europe. They were the lowest caste of European society, restricted in where they could live or what they could do. Jews were often the scapegoats whenever anything went wrong. If there was a disease, the Jews were blamed. If famine hit the area, the Jews were responsible. Jews were accused of poisoning wells, murdering babies, and worse.

But, for Jews, Poland was better than most countries. The Jews in Poland essentially became the merchant class – almost like a medieval middle-class. There was a leader of ancient Poland by the name of Boleslaus the Pious, Prince of Great Poland. In the year 1264, Boleslaus issued a document called the General Charter of Jewish Liberties. In those days, that charter granted all Jews living in Poland the freedom to worship, to trade and to travel. That was a remarkable thing in medieval Europe. So Jews settled in Poland because they had about as much freedom and tolerance as any place that they could find in Europe.

Over the next several hundred years the Jewish situation in Poland fluctuated between tolerance (most of the time) and persecution (some of the time). Because of the general tolerance they experienced in Poland, millions of Jews were living in that country at the time of the Nazi invasion. They tried to defend their country of choice as much as any Pole. During the Nazi invasion of Poland in September of 1939, it is estimated that some 120,000 Polish citizens of Jewish descent took part in those battles as part of the Polish armed forces, first against Germany and then a few weeks later against the Soviet invasion. It was all for nothing because the mechanized armies of Germany and of Russia quickly swept through Poland. The Poles, although they had a large and brave army with an heroic military history, were still fighting with cavalry and lances. The horse-mounted cavalry didn't do much harm to the tanks and airplanes that swept through Poland.

My parents and their families before them came from Poland. My father was born Hersch Laib Rosenberg. Hersch is the Yiddish word for deer or stag and Laib is the Yiddish word for lion. At the time my father came over to the United States in the 1940's all these weird sounding Yiddish immigrant names were changed; in this case Hersch Laib was anglicized to Harry. Harry Truman, at the time, was the President of the United States – so "Harry" was a common and popular replacement name for anything in Yiddish that began with the letter "H".

My mother's name was Feigle, which means little bird in Yiddish. Feigle Schweitzer. When she went through Ellis Island, Feigle became Fay. The name Rosenberg, my father's family name, means Mountain of Roses or Rose Mountain or Rose Castle, take your pick. Schweitzer, the family name of my mother's side, means person from Switzerland.

My father was born in 1914 in a small town in Poland by the name of Bedzin. My mother was born in that same town in 1922. Bedzin has a current population of about 70,000 people. It's located in southeast Poland, in Slaskie Province on the Czarna Przemsza River, a tributary of the Vistula. The town is a heavy industry and coal mining center. It has a long history. It was actually founded in the 14th century. There are the ruins of a 13th century castle in that town. It was a major town on the Warsaw-Krakow trade route. Like most places in Poland it was passed back and forth between countries. Bedzin was passed to Prussia in 1795, then to Russia in 1850 and then back to Poland in 1919.

There was a concentration camp near Bedzin during WWII where at least 10,000 of the town's citizens were murdered. Interestingly enough, Bedzin had a higher population in the 1930's than it has today – an indication that Bedzin has never fully recovered from the horrors of WWII. In the 1930's Bedzin had a population of about 75,000 people. A bit more than a third of that population was Jewish.

At the start of WWII the Jewish population of Bedzin was somewhere between 25,000 and 27,000 people. The Germans occupied Bedzin quickly on September 4, 1939, soon after their Blitzkrieg invasion. They renamed the town as Germans tend to do with conquered cities, calling it Bendsburg. Deportations to Auschwitz began in May of 1942. Before the deportations began, the Jewish population was herded into ghettos. The final liquidation of the Bedzin ghetto started on August 1, 1943.

Bedzin had been a popular town for Jewish settlement because it was on a major trade route and, over the centuries, it had became an important trade and industrial center. Trade and business was one of the very few endeavors the Jews were permitted to engage in, and so settlement in a town on a trade route made good sense to the Jewish population. When one talks about trade and industry in Poland, one really does refer to the Jewish population because it was the Jews, for many centuries, who founded and developed trade and industry in Bedzin and most of Poland. Trading, large trading companies, wholesale, retail businesses, even small industries for the most part were in Jewish hands in Poland.

In 1941 Polish refugees from surrounding areas were streaming into Bedzin. So, because of the refugees escaping even more sordid venues, Bedzin found itself flush with approximately 40,000 Jews. That was more than half the total town population at that time.

Before the outbreak of WWII the Jews and the Gentiles in Bedzin seemed to get along pretty well. At least they tolerated one another and did not seek to repress each other. Interestingly enough, many of the Gentiles worked in Jewish homes over the Sabbath. My parents would tell me that in the Jewish homes starting on Friday night going into Saturday – that is the Jewish Sabbath – Jews were not permitted to work and so they hired Gentiles who would do everything: start the fire in the stove, turn on the gaslights, clean, and do all the work around the house. Jews were not permitted to do any work during the Sabbath. The meals were all cooked ahead of time and they would be served by the Gentiles during the Jewish Sabbath. So there was an interesting symbiotic relationship between the Jews and Gentiles in Bedzin. This is the town in which my parents grew up.

Even though Hersch Laib and Feigle grew up in the same town, they didn't really know each other very well. My parents told me that they had seen each other from time to time, but they were not close. Of course, there was a substantial age difference between my mother and my father. They didn't date while they were living in Bedzin.

At the outbreak of WWII my mother was a teenager. My father was in his mid-twenties. My mother was a schoolgirl. My father, who had never really had much schooling, was in the Polish army. My father's family was a small one: just his father (whose name was David – hence my namesake), his mother (Rachel) and one sister. My mother's family was much larger. Her father's name was Moishe and mother Frieda Schweitzer. She had sisters, Paula and Genya, a brother, Newta, and another brother, Josel. Feigle, my mother, was the youngest of the children.

When the Nazis invaded, my parents and their families – like all other Jews – were herded into the ghettos of Bedzin and remained there for years. In the 1940's however, the Jews were slowly being shipped out to concentration camps and slave labor camps. My father's family was killed by the Nazis. His mother, his father, and his sister were killed. He is the only survivor in his family and was one of only 100,000 Jews liberated from the concentration camps in 1945 by the allies.

My mother's large family was virtually wiped out. The only other family member surviving the Holocaust was her brother Josel who we knew as Uncle Joe. Again, my mother and Uncle Joe were among the 100,000 survivors liberated by the allies in 1945.

Neither my mother nor my father talked very much about their years in Poland or their years in the concentration camps. I think the memories were too stark, horrific and difficult for them and I'm sure they repressed them to a great extent. In fact, my father never, ever talked about his life before the war or during the war. My mother only talked about it fleetingly and only when pressed. I know they both had the blue numbers tattooed on their forearms by the Nazis; a de-humanizing reminder that they were a mere number, less than cattle.

My father also had a deep scar on his forehead – my mother told me that it was the result of a beating he had received from a Kapo. Kapos were other inmates who were put in charge of inmates. In many ways the Kapos were worse than the Nazis. They got special privileges and they lorded it over the other folks in the camps. And they could be cruel.

My parents were young and strong and so they were in labor camps during the war. They probably survived the war because of their strength, both physical and mental. They saw their families killed and sent to the ovens. My mother told me of a harrowing story where one day in her barracks – a barracks of about 200 women – she was sick resting on a lower bunk when an upper bunk mattress fell down on top of her. She said she was too weak to move it and she heard a lot of commotion in the barracks. Apparently the guards and Kapos came in and cleared out the entire barracks that day and sent the whole barracks to the ovens. The Kapo in charge of the barracks later came into the barracks, and found my mother, the only survivor. Thinking it was a miracle, she took my mother under her wing and protected her for quite some time.

Another incident my mother told me about occurred when the guards and kapos were herding people to the ovens and my mother slipped away and hid in the ashes of persons who had been in the ovens. She survived and crept back to the barracks. So, I think it is a series of these sorts of harrowing escapes which allowed my parents to be among the few survivors.

At the conclusion of WWII, the incoming allied troops found concentration camps filled with sick, half-dead human skeletons who had survived the war and the hell of those camps. The guards had fled. My parents – Hersh Laib and Feigle – were there. They were no longer in Poland, having been shipped to camps in Germany. And so, when the allies liberated the camps, my parents found themselves in Germany – Bavaria to be exact – without money, without family, without education, in poor health and alone.

The only family photo in my possession that predates my birth. It is a photo of my mother's family taken before the birth of my mother who was the youngest of the children of David and Rachel Schweitzer. My Uncle Joe is the young man in the very front center of the photo. I estimate the date of this photograph to be 1920.

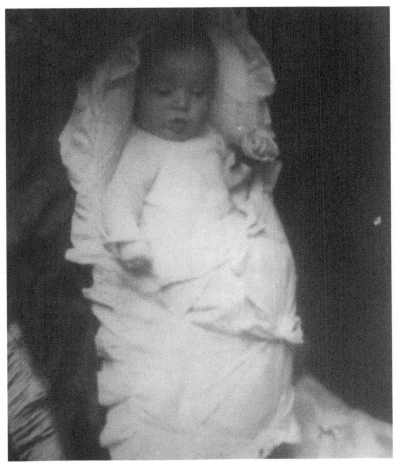

This is the earliest-known photograph of me, probably taken in 1947 in Muenchberg, Germany.

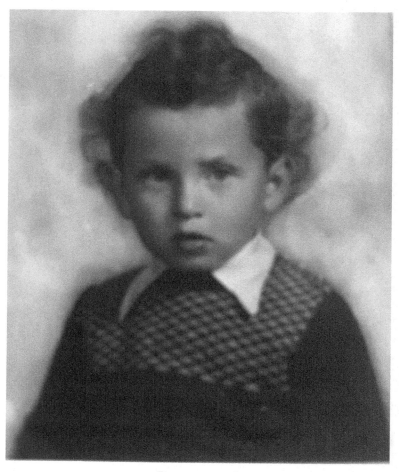

Dave at age 2

The earliest photo of me with my father, Harry Rosenberg. Looks like a sunny day in Bavaria. I believe this photo was taken in 1948, perhaps a year before we left Germany and traveled to the United States.

Two

New York City

Samuel Ellis, a Welshman, immigrated to the American Colonies in the 1700's and settled on a tiny island at the mouth of the Hudson River in New York Harbor, which later bore his name. Mr. Ellis ran a small tavern on the island and served the local fishermen. I bet that good times were had in Mr. Ellis' tavern. Years later, the island was dramatically expanded by landfill and grew to encompass 32 acres. The Federal Government took over Mr. Ellis' Island and from 1892 to 1954 ran it as the main European immigrant processing center for the United States. Today, it's a museum. Interestingly enough, Ellis Island is closely identified with New York, but in actuality over 80% of Ellis Island lies within the boundaries of Jersey City, New Jersey. It's estimated that at least 12 million immigrants saw their first glimpse of America through this center. My parents and I were among these 12 million.

My father's Yiddish name was Hersh Laib; my mother's name was Faigle. In Yiddish, Hersh Laib means stag lion – a nice strong name. In Yiddish, Faigle is translated as little bird – a gentle, pretty name. Of course, when we landed at Ellis Island in 1949 – along with millions of other immigrants from Europe and other venues – everyone got a new, American name. The immigration workers made sure that each name was Americanized, although in their special sense of proportionality they made sure that the first letters of the names generally stayed the same. So, Faigle – at the flick of a pen – became Fay. And, Hersh Laib became Harry – Harry Truman was the President in 1949 otherwise I'm sure Hersh Laib would have become Herschel or Herman. Rosenberg was, apparently, "American" enough (after all, the general who won the war was named Eisenhower) so that name stayed the same. Many an immigrant with last names like Constantinopoulos found their names changed to Poulos. But Rosenberg survived the process. And my name, David (although pronounced "Doo – vid" in Yiddish), was certainly American enough to make it, intact, through the Ellis Island processing center.

I don't have many recollections of New York City. When we arrived I was about three years old. My memories of New York City are the combination of stories my parents told me, old photos, and small flashes of childhood recollections.

I was born on November 20, 1946. My mother and father were living in the small Bavarian village ("Dorf") of Muenchberg at the time of my birth. This village was near the slightly larger hamlet of Hof, located quite close to the border with the Soviet-controlled "eastern zone" which morphed into Soviet-controlled East Germany. Bavaria ("Bayern" in German), of course, was in the zone controlled by the United States. Germany had been divided into four zones by the Allies. The Soviets controlled the eastern portion. The British were principally in the north. The French had a section in the southwest of Germany. And the United States controlled a large swath in the south, particularly Bavaria. The capital city of Berlin, in the middle of the Soviet zone, was also divided into four sectors. Although my parents were, of course, penniless when they were liberated, the Americans imposed a quick remedy. US troops, shocked and disgusted by what they had found in the liberated concentration camps, simply "liberated" German businesses from the Germans. When they found a business run by Germans which had not been bombed to oblivion, the Americans just dispossessed them and installed a Jewish family. Apparently, that's what happened with my parents. My father, compliments of the American troops, suddenly found himself as the general director of a small factory that produced textiles – yarn and cloth. My father called it the "Weberei" which is a Yiddish term for weaving mill. He didn't know anything about that sort of business, but he was industrious and for close to three years he ran that company, earned a living, and saved a little money.

In 1949, my mother, father and I came to New York City because my mother wanted to get out of Germany, and because my mother's brother Joe, the only surviving member of her family, had moved to New York City a year or two earlier. While Joe didn't tell my parents that the streets were paved with gold, apparently he told them that good opportunities awaited those who were willing to work in America. In fact, New York City was the first stop for virtually all Jews and other immigrants from Europe. Most of them wound up staying right there. Some of them – like my parents and I – eventually moving on to New Jersey. But first there was New York.

We had come to America with some money. My father had sold the weaving mill in Muenchberg and so we had a nest-egg. Those immigrants who came with money were processed through Ellis Island in a relatively short time – a matter of hours usually. Those who came penniless had to wait, or might even be sent back to their countries of origin. We processed through. None of us spoke a word of English, of course, but with the help of Joe and other friends from Europe who had preceded us, we settled into a rather nice apartment. My father, now called Harry, took up work as a butcher – although he called himself a businessman – and my mother, Fay, stayed home with me. The sights, sounds and smells of New York City have stayed with me my entire life. I remember walking the streets of the city with my mother on brisk days and seeing bagel vendors hawking their warm bagels. Bagels are those quintessentially Jewish, round boiled, then baked little breads that have a hole in the middle, and the bagel vendors were selling them stacked up on long sticks. Selling warm bagels from a stick on the street may be a relic of the past, but for a little boy of three or four, nothing could surpass munching on that fragrant, warm, slightly crusty and chewy bagel.

There were no supermarkets in the early 1950's. Every product was sold from a specialty shop. There was the milk market, the bakery, the butcher shop, the egg lady, the fish market, the vegetable and fruit stand, and so on. My mother spent most of her day, every day shopping, going from market to market and shop to shop, sniffing, poking, and testing the various items to pick only the best. It was, indeed, a time-consuming process, but it was also a social process. In between shopping, my mother would chat with her friends from the neighborhood, or joke around with the vendors. Of all the markets I visited with my mother, the fish market stands out in my memory. You could smell the fish market the very moment you crossed the threshold. And once inside, you were in a different world. It was a world all in white tile, containing many mysterious tanks of salt and fresh water, each of them were filled with fish and exotic creatures of the sea, lake and river. When you went in the market and found a fish you wanted, you would point it out and the fish monger – dressed all in white like a surgeon at a fancy hospital – would quickly net it out of the water and immediately take it over to a tile table and whack it on the head with a large mallet. He would then proceed to cut it up precisely the way you wanted it cut up. You sure don't see that nowadays, but that's the way they did it in those days. My mother was a pretty good cook, and our meals normally revolved around chicken or fish. Every now and then some lamb, and rarely beef which was expensive and not that readily available in New York. I learned my cooking skills from my mother. My father was a pretty good eater. He could consume the gamut of food from carp (he loved the eyes for some reason), herring, boiled potatoes with sour cream (a Polish dish which was his favorite), anchovies on toast, brains and eggs. I did not share my father's rather eclectic taste buds.

I have a distinct memory of our first television set. This television set must have been purchased by my parents in 1950, soon after the television age started. The furniture in my apartment was good furniture – cherry mahogany was all the rage in those days – and so everything in our apartment was made of fine cherry mahogany with lion's paws at the end of curved legs and metal rings in the noses of the lions. The television set was, in fact, a piece of furniture also made out of cherry mahogany. The set was mostly considered furniture because there was hardly any programming on in those days – just a few hours a day. Most of the time all we saw was a test signal screen with a constant tone. In fact, there were occasions when we would watch the test signal and listen to the tone, just because television was such a miraculous thing. It was a remarkably big set with a remarkably tiny television screen.

My favorite show, by far, was the Howdy Doody Show. I would watch that show with religious regularity. Howdy Doody, of course, was the star. Howdy was a perpetually-smiling freckle-faced puppet in a plaid western-style shirt, actually, a marionette with very visible strings. The live person on the show was a slightly rotund, middle-aged wannabe cowboy named Buffalo Bob. There were also live kids on the show who sat – and cheered – in the "peanut gallery". Buffalo Bob would start the show by saying "Hi ya kids, what time is it?" And the kids would always yell back in unison, "It's Howdy Doody time!" Sitting at home, I would also yell back, "It's Howdy Doody time!" And my mother, in the kitchen, would then yell – in slightly broken English, "It's Howdy Doody time!" As much as television has shaped American culture, it also helped me – and to some extent my parents – understand America and learn our new language. Another marionette on that show was the rail thin Dilly Dally, that's Howdy's best friend, who was kind of a stupid guy but that was obvious as he was given buck teeth. There was the dandified mayor of the town, Phinneus T. Bluster. And there was a beautiful Indian Princess, called Princess Summer Fall Winter Spring. There was a clown, the other live person on the show, Clarabelle. Clarabelle would honk his horn but never said a word on that show. If he wanted to speak, Clarabelle would write a note. It was all in good clean fun. The adventures of Howdy Doody. I never missed a show.

As I reflect back on my life in New York City it seemed to me that we lived pretty well. We had a nice apartment on a high floor. We had good furniture. When my father sold his textile factory in Bavaria he clearly brought some money with him to New York City.

I believe that my first actual, unaided memory as a child came from New York City. I recall riding a tricycle down the sidewalk with my mother. I remember a little boy coming up to me and speaking to me – but the sounds he made were mere gibberish to my ears. As I reflect back on this I realize the little boy was talking to me in English, and I didn't understand a word he was saying because I did not speak English having been brought up in Germany. I spoke a mixture of Yiddish and German and Polish. I think he was asking me if he could ride my tricycle. I remember being very frustrated because all I heard from the boy was blah-blah-blah.

I have memories of playing with other little boys in a vacant lot on small hills – probably piles of rubbish – near my apartment. We had made some wooden swords. That's all a boy really needs. It seems to me we played for hours with those wooden swords, racing up and down the hills making believe we were knights of the realm, pirates, or cavalry soldiers. All it takes is a wooden sword.

Summers in New York City could be brutal. Heat and humidity. Sometimes my mother would draw me a cold water bath, just to cool down. No one had air conditioning, so we opened the windows at night to let in a trickle of warm air. We would dampen our bed sheets with tap water to cool them off. When it got unbearably hot, we would either go to Coney Island or to the Catskills.

There is a peninsula in New York in the very south of Brooklyn called Coney Island, bordered by Brighton Beach and Manhattan Beach to the east, Seagate to the west, Gravesend to the north and the Atlantic Ocean to the south. It actually used to be an island and got its name from the Dutch settlers of New Amsterdam who called it Conyne Eylandt (rabbit island) since it was overrun with rabbits. Hunting rabbits was the thing to do on Coney Island until the resorts and amusements were built. People came in and the rabbits went away. The first carousel – carved by hand – was built and started operating in Coney Island in 1876. Rail lines were laid. The bathhouses followed. Nathan's Famous Hot Dogs made its appearance in 1916. New Yorkers flocked to the Coney Island beach. Some time after World War II, Coney Island started a downward spiral from which it never recovered.

But, in the early 1950's before the street gangs scared everyone away, on a hot summer day, Coney Island was still the place to go and its beach was normally jam packed. One had to step gingerly around bodies and blankets. And that's where my mother, father and I would go to escape the stifling heat. It is amazing how many tens of thousands of people can jam into Coney Island and onto the sandy beach. My recollection of Coney Island is wall-to-wall people. Everyone staked out their little space on the sand, delineated by their blanket. That was their claimed property, like the Spaniards claiming land for Queen Isabella. There wasn't a whole lot of space around those blankets. Hardly anyone owned a bathing suit in those days. If you went to Coney Island and wanted to use the beach or a bath house, you would rent a bathing suit. Rental booths were everywhere. You would pay the clerk some money and he would give you a bathing suit on a hanger. You would go into a dressing room, put on the bathing suit and bring back the hanger with your clothes on it and hand it to the clerk. The clerk gave you a ticket. Fair trade – you traded your clothes for the bathing suit and if you decided you didn't want to turn in the bathing suit I guess you lost your clothes. But in any event that's how you got a bathing suit on Coney Island.

The suits were a little strange and never fit perfectly well. They were constructed of a kind of natural fabric material so that when they got wet they got pretty stretchy. But everyone was wearing the exact same kind of stretchy bathing suit so that was fine. There were dozens of these bathing suit rental places along the Coney Island and heaven help you if you forgot which rental place held your clothes. After you put on your suit, before you got to the beach you had to walk through these huge public showers and one-foot deep wading pools. I suppose it was kind of a sanitation thing but you had to go through that before you got to the beach and the ocean.

One day at Coney Island, I somehow got separated from my mother in that public shower room. For a child of four, it was a scary experience I still remember to this day. I don't know how long I was separated from my mother but it was frightening. Suddenly, it seemed to me that there was water everywhere. I couldn't figure out what was up and what was down. I kept falling over. I felt like I was drowning. I couldn't breathe. I vaguely remember someone pulling me out of the water and eventually helping me find my mother. Somehow I think the police were involved but I don't really recall for sure. I just remember being very happy to reconnect with my mother again and I made sure to stay pretty close to her when we went to Coney Island on our future trips.

Today, New York's Jewish families go to Florida in the summer. In the 1950's, those who could afford it would go to the Catskill Mountains, or as it was generally known simply "the Catskills". The Catskill Mountains are located northwest of New York City and southwest of Albany. Geologically speaking, they aren't mountains at all, but simply higher ground. But to the Jewish families who flocked there to escape the summer humidity of New York City, they were the Jewish Alps. All sorts of Jewish resorts catered to the New York City crowd – Brown's, Grossinger's and many others. So many Jewish musicians and comedians got their start in the Catskills that the area became known as "the Borscht Belt." These giants of Jewish comedy included Red Buttons, Joey Bishop, Sid Caesar, Groucho Marx, Woody Allen, Victor Borge, Rodney Dangerfield, Don Rickles, Phil Silvers, Jack Benny, Gene Wilder, Danny Kaye, Henny Youngman, Milton Berle, and many, many others. And from time to time, my parents and I, with all our friends, would caravan up to the Catskills for a week of living large. The women would wear their sun suits and play cards all day. The men would wear their best leisure suits with shirt collars splayed, smoke cigarettes, drink Schnapps, and talk about Poland. The kids, in shorts and cowboy gear, spent all day running up and down the hills, guns blazing, searching for the elusive Indians who hid behind every bush and tree. Evenings were spent together dining on fine fare – always with cantaloupe (somehow, in the Catskills, cantaloupe was an ethnic favorite) – and being entertained by the finest musicians and comedians in the world. We slept like the dead. This was high living.

At the end of an exhausting week full of good food and good memories, we traveled back to New York to sweat again in the heat of the city.

I had two particular friends in New York, also the sons of recent immigrants. One of them was named Peter, a bit older than me, and the other boy, about my age, we called Harry, because his real name was Heino, and no self-respecting American kid wanted to be known as Heino. Peter was the distinguished member of our group as he was the first to sprout a pubic hair, which resulted in numerous wrestling matches as we all tried to locate it. Harry and Peter and I would hang out a lot whenever our parents got together. Peter's father was a thick-necked man with a huge belly and large hairy forearms. Harry's father was a skinny fellow with a scraggly mustache. The parents would go off into one room to discuss whatever it was adults discussed and we boys would go into another room to play, or we would play in the lobby of the apartment house where we gathered. This was the little group of immigrants who had known each other from their days of liberation in Germany after the war and they had all eventually moved to New York City.

We pretty much hung out with each other. We had minimal contact with the Americans and others. Like most ethnic groups – Irish, Italians, Puerto Ricans, Jews, Blacks, etc. – in the 1950's we would hang out with our "own kind". As it turned out we wound up only spending a short time in New York City, perhaps only a year or a year and a half, but from time to time, we would travel back to New York and visit with our old friends.

*I remember walking along the hard pavement of New York
City with my mother and seeing this pony and a street
photographer. The rest is history. The happy boy is me
somewhere around the age of four. It must have been 1950.*

*My beautiful mother, Fay Rosenberg, with me in the Catskills.
Notice that I already have my eye on some of my friends in
the distance. And notice the cowboy sweater.*

Three

The Farm

It seems that my Uncle Joe Schweitzer, the man who had urged us to come to the United States, prevailed upon my father to buy a farm for him. Joe had decided that he wanted to leave New York City and he wanted to go to New Jersey and be a farmer. Specifically, because he had been in the butcher business and knew something about chickens, he wanted a chicken farm in New Jersey. So my father, at the insistence of my mother, went out and bought a chicken farm for Uncle Joe. I have no idea how much he paid for it but it was a pretty big chicken farm with coops and a ranch with thousands of chickens.

But then a strange thing happened. After money changed hands and the farm was purchased by my father at the request of Uncle Joe and the urgings of my mother, Uncle Joe had a change of heart. I heard about this for years and years and years and it was a major bone of contention between my father and my mother. Uncle Joe changed his mind and decided he did not want to be a farmer after all. But the die was cast. And so my father, my mother and I wound up becoming owners of a chicken ranch. You can't raise chickens long distance, so we moved to the chicken ranch in New Jersey. Ironically, a couple of years later, Uncle Joe and his family also moved to New Jersey, but they weren't running the chicken ranch. We were. Even though Joe and his family lived fairly close to us in New Jersey, my father refused to see them, and it was a decade before we finally paid them a visit, my father speaking perhaps 10 words during the entire sojourn.

So, around 1951, we became farmers. We moved to New Jersey to a ranch near Vineland in Southern New Jersey. New Jersey is thought of as being a very urban area but much of it is quite rural, and there are many small farms particularly in Southern

Jersey. We lived on that farm for a bit over four years. Overnight I went from being a city boy to becoming a farm boy.

Our farm was in an extremely rural area. We had no immediate neighbors. Our farm was divided by a dirt country road – on one side of the road was our large chicken ranch, and on the other side was our house, the hired-hand's shack, the barn and the chicken coops. Going in one direction on the road, one had to travel a good mile to find our "next-door" neighbor, another farmer. Traveling the other direction on the road for a mile, one would eventually get to the junction of a paved highway. At that very junction stood a graveyard, a small church and the elementary school I attended. In fact, between our farm and the schoolhouse, there was no living person.

Our farmhouse was actually a remarkable building. It was a massive old stone building, probably a hundred years old. That was where we lived. Close to the stone building was a small shack that was used by our hired hand – we almost always had a hired hand – typically a black man. Behind the shack where our hired hand lived we had five or six chicken coops where many young chickens resided and there were also coops for the hatchlings. We had equipment with lots of internal light bulbs which created the heat necessary so the eggs could hatch into chicks. Across the dirt road from our house was a large ranch where four to five thousand birds lived in open coops, surrounded by high fences.

We, of course, had a barn. That's where my father slaughtered the chickens. We also had a chicken plucking machine that was based on the principal of lots of steam. The recently slaughtered chickens would go in with feathers and come out without them. In the basement of our house we had a candling operation. Let me tell you about the candling machine because I spent many, many days as a small child working that candling machine. On a farm, everyone works.

The first candling machines – prior to electric lights – actually used candles, hence their name. The machine was constructed in such a way that the eggs would roll downward, propelled by gravity past the candle (or in our case an electric light) so that the worker on the machine could see through the lit egg to determine if the egg had any blood in it. If the egg had blood in it, it would go into a separate pile. Nothing is wasted on a farm. Those eggs were still sold, but very cheaply. There were people who buy those eggs because they were dirt cheap. In addition to checking the eggs for any blood, the machine would weigh eggs. They would roll into various chutes depending on their size. You had the jumbos, you had the extra large and the large, the medium and the small, you had the peewees and you had the eggs with double yolks. These would all be sorted by size and put into separate containers because they were sold for different prices. And yes, when I was in kindergarten, first grade, second grade and third grade, I would work the candling machine. Like most farm families everyone had to do some work. My mother would feed the chickens, the hired hand would do the heavy work, my father would go to town and make the deals like all good Jewish fathers, and I would work the candling machine.

My first school was a one-room schoolhouse, just like Abe Lincoln I imagined. This was a schoolhouse which housed kindergarten, first, second and third grades, all in one room with one teacher. We had about 30 kids at any given time. The room was heated in winter with one pot-belly stove that stood smack in the middle. In the morning on cold days all of us kids would bring potatoes that we would throw into the oven. At lunch we would pull out a potato, which may or may not be the one we brought, and that would be part of our lunch. Even though we had just one room, four different grades, and one teacher, and no fancy trappings, seems like I got a decent education. But school wasn't the highlight of my day. Getting to and from school was.

On a few occasions I would get a ride, typically from the hired hand in an old truck, but normally I had to walk to and from school. My mother didn't drive because my father never thought it was important that she do so. He was very old school about such things. It was a long walk, about a mile each way. And it was a scary walk because there was no one between my house and the school. The dirt road was desolate and flanked by deep woods.

When I left the boundaries of my farm, I entered the forbidden zone of the woods. My child's imagination put an exclamation point on every sound, or worse, lack of sound. I literally had to walk — sometimes run — down that dirt road through the woods to get to my school. Worse, just before the schoolhouse was a deserted cemetery — I never saw another human there — which was the coup de grace of horror for a small boy. On cold, windy days there were occasions I actually ran home just to stay one step ahead of the murderers and the ghosts, but that's how I got to school and that's how I got home.

But don't get me wrong. Growing up on a farm is actually a lot of fun. We had a black dog that we (in an imaginative moment) named Blackie, and Blackie and I had the run of the farm. I never had any friends over, because we had no neighbors. So Blackie and I would play in the woods, we would play in the barn, or near the coops, or in an old junked, tireless car that squatted near the barn. I played with a tin can and a stick and used that like a shot put to launch that tin can and the dog would chase the can and bring it back to me. Tarzan was big on television in those days and, stripping down to my underwear, Blackie and I would play the King of the Jungle. Simple pleasures.

Connected to the front of the house was a big veranda which ran the length of the house and was open and airy with windows and screens. There was an old phonograph on the veranda that actually worked from time to time, and would play 78 records. I'm not talking about 33 or 45 records, but the big, heavy 78 records. I would listen to the sounds of the 1930's and 1940's while playing on the veranda. One of my favorite childhood games was to ride my tricycle on the veranda. I would imagine that I was a bus driver stopping at various stations on the veranda to pick up and drop off passengers. I was pretty good at the sounds of the big bus, and the shoosh of opening and closing the bus door, taking clattering change in the bus till. As I child I did not dream of growing up to be a firefighter or a policeman. I dreamed of being a bus driver. Isolated as I was on the farm the thought of driving a big bus seemed like a high calling for me.

I had a wonderful bedroom on the second floor of the old farmhouse. It was small but I remember being very cozy in that room. There were always a couple of big comforters on the bed so I stayed warm on the coldest nights. Even though my bedroom was small, I had a huge parlor right outside my bedroom filled with my toys. I had a big toy chest and spent lots and lots of time with my toys. For some reason my favorite toys were the soldiers. I could literally spend hours up in that parlor on the second floor playing with the toy soldiers – setting up armies engaged in endless battles.

Life wasn't easy on the farm – life was difficult because money was tight. I remember my father complaining bitterly about Dwight Eisenhower and the Republicans and their farm administration which, in his opinion, was terrible for farmers. We weren't doing so well financially and my father whose temper was short in any event would sometimes completely lose that temper and give me a good whipping. As a result of some indiscretion inevitably committed by a small boy, he would completely lose his composure and, frothing slightly, would chase me through the house. Sometimes my mother would intervene, and sometimes she couldn't stop him. If he caught me – and he usually did – I would get a severe paddling. Nowadays probably it would be considered child abuse, but in those days it was just father disciplining son.

On only one occasion while on the farm do I recall ever spending time at a neighbor's home. There came a day when both my parents had to go to Vineland to take care of some business. My mother made arrangements for me to stay at the home of one of my classmates – a blond boy whose name was Donald Ay. I was to spend several hours at the Ay home, and even have dinner with the Ay family. They lived about two miles from our farmhouse next to the highway. For me, it was like a trip to a foreign land, particularly the dinner. Before we ate, everyone said grace – which was a new one on me. I didn't really know what to do, but I had the presence of mind to bow my head. When the food was served, it was served family style and we all passed the serving plates. There was mashed potatoes, which I recognized, of course. And then there was some sort of meat that I had never seen before. It was ham. I had not seen ham before as a Jewish boy. In retrospect, I wonder if they served ham that evening just because the Jewish boy was staying at their house.

My father decided around 1954 that he had had enough of farm life. Frankly, he wasn't on the farm all that much. Every free chance he had he would head into the city. The largest and closest city to our farm was Atlantic City. Father decided in 1954 that we were going to move to Atlantic City.

Just prior to our move to Atlantic City – while we still lived on the farm – I remember two great events that occurred. First, we became citizens of the United States, and second I moved into a brand new school.

We had moved to the United States in 1949. In those days, one could become citizens in five years, and we did. I helped my parents study for their tests on America and by some miracle, they passed! My mother and father and I dressed up in our best clothes and went to the county seat in Vineland. They received their citizenship papers in 1954, and I (as an eight year old) became a citizen automatically. I once had a Polaroid photo – in faded color – of mother and father proudly holding their citizenship certificates.

The second great event in my farm life was the new school. One day, I was amazed to learn that the school district trustees had built themselves a brand new school building. I was to be among the first students to move into that new school although – with our impending move to Atlantic City – I was only able to spend a short time there in the third grade. But I had some fond memories of that new school. There's nothing quite like a new school building. Everything is clean. The smell of the school, the paint, the brick, the concrete, the wood – all those new smells were wonderful. We were able to house all the different grades – kindergarten through sixth grade for the whole area in this school and every grade had its own classroom – that in and of itself seemed like a remarkable thing. So we had seven classrooms in this school – one for each grade and the kindergartners, each with their own teachers.

All the books were new, all the supplies were new. I remember the distinctive smell of the crayons. I remember the pre-printed tests they gave us on off-white paper with dark green ink, which was so different from the black and white stuff that I'd seen up to that point. They had white boards in the new school, not the outmoded black boards. Everything was new and different and I loved going to school.

I remember planting a bean. The whole class planted beans in a glass jars full of dirt. Beans grow very, very fast and that was impressive to me. You could even see the roots through the glass. And at a certain point the bean pod would open. Science became real for me with that bean.

School for me was a great escape from the house and I ate up every minute of it. And no more walking. The yellow bus would pick me up every day, and drop me off right at home. It was also the one occasion I could play with some other kids, being very isolated back on the farm.

When I was in the third grade at this new school I got hit in the head. We were playing pretty roughly in the yard, near the out buildings at the school and some of the kids had climbed up on the outhouses and were throwing rocks and cans and other objects at the other kids and we were attacking them – stupid stuff – and a can hit me on the back of the head. I got a pretty nasty cut. I remember my mother being called and I remember us racing off to the closest town, Vineland, to see the doctor. Sure enough I had to get stitches right in the doctor's office. Not a happy experience for someone who is in the third grade. And I have a scar behind my right ear to prove it, although it is under the hairline so no one has ever seen it. When my father learned that I had been hit in the head, he grunted and said it was probably a good thing as it might knock some "Zeichel" (intelligence) into my head.

Whether or not that can knocked some Zeichel into me is as yet unknown. But at the end of my third grade year my parents and I disposed of the farm. I suspect my father took a financial loss on the farmstead. He sold the whole thing – lock, stock, barrel and candling machine – and we moved to Atlantic City, New Jersey. We arrived in Atlantic City toward the end of 1954, beginning of 1955.

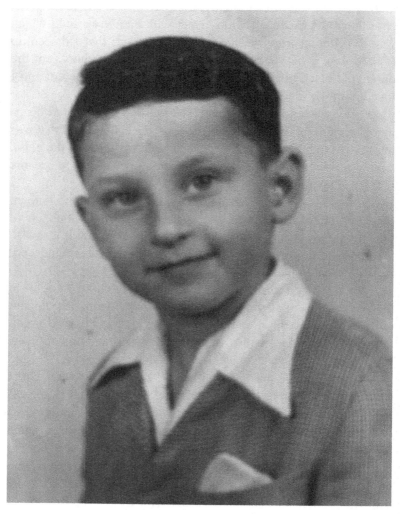

Dave at age 7

Four

A Brief History of Atlantic City

Mention Atlantic City and most people have a particular mental picture: boardwalk, sand, ocean, beaches, Steel Pier, Monopoly, Atlantic Ocean, Miss America, tourists, casinos. It's all of that, and more. Atlantic City is actually located on an island in South Jersey, called Abescon Island. Although most folks who live in Atlantic City probably don't know that.

It seems that Atlantic City has always been a resort town. The original inhabitants of the area were the Lenni-Lenape Indians. It is said that the Leni-Lenapes would leave the mainland each year and travel down a five-mile-long trail called, appropriately, the Old Indian Trail, which crossed the marshland to Abescon Island. They made the trek so that they could spend their summers on the island, hunting, fishing and relaxing. What the Indians knew, the European settlers soon discovered. After Europeans came to America, the island was visited not only by the Indians, but also by hunters, trappers, fishermen, and a few hardy, early settlers.

The first non-Indian to build a permanent residence on Abescon Island was said to be Jeremiah Leeds who built himself a home and a farm in 1785. Not much happened for the next three or four generations. In 1850 there were only seven permanent dwellings on the island, all but one of which was owned by the descendants of Jeremiah Leeds. That one belonged to Dr. Jonathan Pitney, a physician who, with Richard Osborne, a civil engineer from Philadelphia, came up with the idea to bring a rail line into the island. And so, in 1854 a profound thing happened to Abescon Island which would change its character forever. In that year, specifically on July 5, 1854, the first train arrived from Camden, New Jersey. And with it, the first tourists.

Richard Osborne is generally given credit for naming this city.

Not a difficult feat. It was a city, of course. And it did sit next to the Atlantic. So, how about Atlantic City? While Mr. Osborne had his epiphany about the name of the town, Dr. Pitney was busy dreaming up names for the new city's streets. Those names, generations later, would be made famous by the board game of "Monopoly". Dr. Pitney decided that the long boulevards which would run parallel to the Atlantic Ocean would bear the names of great oceans and bodies of water: Atlantic, Pacific, Baltic, Arctic, Adriatic and Mediterranean. And the streets that would run perpendicular to the Atlantic Ocean would be named after the states: Texas, Illinois, Indiana, Vermont, Massachusetts, New York and so on.

The early visitors to Atlantic City liked what they found. Balmy summers, clean white sands, good fishing, and literally miles and miles of ocean beaches. They came by train. But they also came by sea. Atlantic City had become a decent port. And then a road was built. The first road – a toll road – from the mainland to the island took 17 years to build out. Construction finished in 1870 and tourists had yet another way to come to Atlantic City. And because it was a toll road – a road that cost money to traverse – an even more affluent set of tourists started the trek to Atlantic City.

Atlantic City was becoming quite the popular destination. Lots of people – rich and not so rich – wanted to get to the strand. By the year 1878, one railroad line simply couldn't handle all the passengers, and a second rail line was constructed. About this time with the influx of sun-seeking tourists, rooming houses and hotels started to emerge on the island. Some of the new hotels were massive, in the scale of Grand Hotels, taking up entire city blocks and sporting the latest in luxury and – for the time – modern amenities. The hotels and hotel dining rooms of Atlantic City were all the rage on the East Coast. Post cards sent from Atlantic City were coveted, and Atlantic City produced a lot of postcards.

But there was a problem. The very thing that made Atlantic City the Mecca for summer tourists was becoming the bane of the hotelier's existence: sand. Sand, sand, and more sand. Sand was a problem in restaurants and hotel lobbies. Sand could ruin a floor and damage a carpet. Outdoors, the white sands of Atlantic City were coveted. Indoors, sand was just a nuisance. A train conductor – Alexander Boardman – actually came up with an idea to overcome the problem of sand, and his idea was sold to the city council. Boardman – aptly named – came up with the idea of building a boardwalk from the beach into the town. And so, in 1870, using up half the tax revenues of Atlantic City, and authorized by an enlightened city council, an 8-foot wide boardwalk was built from the beach into the city. What a concept. One could rise above the sand and travel from the beach to the hotels on a walkway of boards. This was, in fact, Atlantic City's first "boardwalk" – a feature that would become the city's icon. In 1880, the original boardwalk was replaced with a larger one. But in 1889, a terrific hurricane (the constant bane of Absecon Island) swept through Atlantic City, destroyed the boardwalk and put the city under some 6-feet of salt water.

Of course, the boardwalk (or as it is known today, the Boardwalk) was rebuilt. Today, the Boardwalk is 60 feet wide and almost 6 miles long. The planks are placed in a herringbone pattern and are supported by steel and concrete. On the landward side, the Boardwalk is ringed with shops and amusements. On the seaward side are the famous piers, jutting fearlessly into the brine: the Steel Pier, the former Million Dollar Pier, the Garden Pier, and Central Pier. Also, at various intervals, rock jetties, like dark fingers, splay into the ocean and create natural separation of the great sand beaches. The world's first Oceanside amusement pier was build in Atlantic City in 1882, called Ocean Pier. Steel Pier opened in 1898 and Million Dollar Pier opened in 1906.

Those piers became a great draw for Atlantic City. One could find the Ripley's Believe-it-or-Not Odditorium, pinball arcades, penny arcades (where some games actually cost one penny), the famous Diving Horse. Atlantic City was the place to go and the place to be. Famous people came to Atlantic City to see and be seen. Atlantic City was near New York and Philadelphia and the summer heat and swelter of the big cities could be escaped with a relatively quick trip to the sun and breezes of the shore. Swank hotels sprang up along the Boardwalk, including the Brighton, the Chelsea, the Shelburne, the Ambassador, the Ritz Carlton, and the Breakers. In 1930, the Claridge opened with 24 stories, known as the "Skyscraper by the Sea", a truly remarkable thing for a town of 25,000 people.

Atlantic City also became known as the home of the Miss America Pageant. Begun in 1921 as a way to keep tourists in the city, Atlantic City and Miss America became – for many years at least – inseparable. The host of the Pageant, Bert Parks and his famous song ("Here she comes, Miss America") became identified with the city, until January of 2006 when the Pageant was moved to Las Vegas.

In 1964, Atlantic City – tiny as it was – hosted the Democratic National Convention which nominated Lyndon Johnson for President and Hubert Humphrey for Vice President. The Democratic ticket won that election in a landslide. But Atlantic City, by that time, had already deteriorated. The tourists had for the most part, stopped coming. The city was changing. Many shops and amusements on the Boardwalk had shut down. By the 1960's, Atlantic City had become known as "Skid Row by the Sea." The population in 2000 was 40,000, 44% of whom were black, 25% Hispanic and 10% Asian, and 26% white. Atlantic City was experiencing all the problems of a major urban area: poverty, crime, loss of jobs, flight by the middle class, deteriorating neighborhoods. In an effort to "save" Atlantic City, New Jersey voters approved casino gambling in 1976 for Atlantic City, and the first casino opened in 1978. But the casinos didn't save Atlantic City.

I visited Atlantic City for a few hours in the early 1980's. It was just a visit to assuage my curiosity. I hadn't been in Atlantic City for about 25 years. I found, to my amazement, a tattered and torn Atlantic City. Virtually everything had changed. Entire blocks were gone. My old apartment on the corner of Atlantic Avenue and New Hampshire Avenue was gone. My old school – the Massachusetts Avenue School – was a bombed out wreck of a building, surrounded by razor wire. The butcher shop my father had run was empty. The toy and magic store next to the butcher shop was now a porn shop. Shops on the Boardwalk were simply gone or boarded up. From time to time, a casino would loom on the Boardwalk – but between the casinos it might as well have been Baghdad or Beirut. The only thing that I could see that had remained the same was the fire station on Atlantic Avenue. The fire fighters were still sitting in their chairs out front, waiting for the call. But that was the 1980's. My memories of Atlantic City were memories of the glory days of that town – the 1950's – those were the years I spent in what was then still a place of significance.

Five

We Move to Atlantic City

We gave up the farm in 1955. I was nine years old. When I say we gave up the farm I mean precisely that. After railing against Dwight Eisenhower and the Republican administration for many, many months, my father decided that raising chickens and candling eggs was just not going to make ends meet. In fact, I may have become a subliminal Democrat about this time since I have many recollections of my father ranting against the Eisenhower administration and what Republicans were doing to small farmers.

In any event I had a feeling that the end to my days on the farm was coming since my father was beginning to take longer and longer trips away from the farm, leaving me and my mother behind. He would go to Atlantic City on these trips. I never knew what he actually did there – these trips were quite mysterious to a boy of nine. But he would be gone for days and then he would return. And nothing was really said about it. Except one day we were packing and moving. My father decided we'd sell the farm. I suspect we took quite a loss, and we moved the entire Rosenberg estate to Atlantic City. Now, as a child of nine, that wasn't a really a very bad thing.

While I enjoyed the farm immensely, Atlantic City in 1955 to a nine year old boy was truly a charmed place. Now, I have to sketch for you the Atlantic City of 1955. It is completely and totally different than the Atlantic City of the 21st Century. The Atlantic City that we presently see is a city of dirt and slums. In places it virtually looks like a war zone. Except for a few prominent casinos, almost everything in between and behind the casinos is slum, slum, slum. But in 1955, Atlantic City was truly a place of mystery and magic, particularly for a boy of nine.

The population of Atlantic City in 1955 was rather small

– fewer than 40,000 people. But, Atlantic City had all the trappings of a big town. Let me tell you what I mean by that. It had really tall buildings – I mean 15-25 story buildings, which are just not found in small towns. It also had a trolley car line on Atlantic Avenue, the Jitney line on Pacific Avenue, and a bus line on Baltic Avenue. I'm sure you have heard of all these avenues because of the game of Monopoly for some reason is modeled after Atlantic City. In any event, Atlantic City has a number of very long avenues, Pacific, Atlantic, Baltic, and these were conducive to public transportation lines. On Pacific Avenue we had the Jitney. The jitney is a little bus – in those days it was blue – that could seat maybe 12 people. You could ride the jitney for a nickel, or you could advance purchase tokens for a nickel to ride the jitney. The beauty of the jitney, it was always running. In other words, when you got on the jitney you could look down the street and you would see another jitney coming. So you never really had to wait. They were constantly running. And the same was true with the trolleys. The trolleys ran on Atlantic Avenue. I tended to ride the jitneys because they were more fun. Between the jitneys of Pacific Avene and the trolleys of Atlantic Avenue and the buses of Baltic Avenue, everything pretty much got connected. Hardly anyone used a car in those days. Public transportation was just too good and too cheap and got you everywhere you wanted to go.

The family and I moved into an apartment building on the southwest corner of New Hampshire and Atlantic Avenue, just two blocks from the boardwalk and four blocks from my elementary school, the three-story Massachusetts Avenue School at the corner of Massachusetts and Atlantic. It was a fairly ramshackle five-story apartment building, built of wood, painted white, with outdoor fire escapes and little outdoor landings to the fire escapes that we used as balconies. On balmy evenings we could all crowd onto the landing and enjoy the salty night air and the sound of the surf. The Rosenberg family set up housekeeping on the fourth floor. Nothing fancy, just four rooms. Moved from the big farm house to the small apartment. But it was plenty. And I still had my own room. I had developed quite the collection of comic books and Mad Magazines. I read the comics voraciously. Comics cost a dime then, and Mad Magazine was only a quarter. I truly believe that I improved my reading skills because of all the comic book reading I did. I loved Superman, but didn't much care for Batman. I read the Phantom (the Ghost Who Walks as he was known), and Blackhawk, Tarzan and the Flash. While in Atlantic City I developed quite the collection of comic books and Mad Magazines which I kept in pristine condition in the closet of my room. I'm sure if I had those comics and magazines today, the collection would be worth tens of thousands of dollars.

Six

My Father, the Butcher;
My Mother, the Seamstress

In our years in Atlantic City, which spanned 1955 to 1958 my father was a butcher. He was the proprietor of his own shop, paying rent with the money he got from the sale of the farm and ultimately from sales of meat and poultry.

I remember the butcher shop very well; it was all tile floors, clean and neat. It had a well-used butcher block that was deeply indented from all the hacking and carving of knives. There were display cabinets full of chickens and meat of various kinds. They would make sausage and hamburger on the spot. Chicken was very popular because it was very cheap. I remember different cuts of meat for different economic strata. The poorest of poor, who were the black folks in town – in those days we called them Negroes – they bought the necks, the backs and the wings. There wasn't much meat on them, but they were real cheap. You could cook them in water and make a soup. The wealthier folks bought the breasts and the thighs and the chicken legs. But the necks and backs and wings, that was the poor man's fare.

My father worked in the butcher shop morning to night. He always had a helper or two. They wore white just like a doctor, and they always had caps on.

But more interesting than the butcher shop was the neighborhood around the butcher shop. We lived only a few blocks away from the butcher shop so I could actually walk there. There was a barber college around the corner where I could get a decent haircut for next to nothing. There was a bar called the Jockey Club, and the windows were always closed as was the door. I saw men come and go into the Jockey Club, which I later learned was a gay bar

– but boys of nine in the 1950's know nothing about such things. The neighborhood immediately around the butcher shop included a toy store and a magic store, believe it or not, immediately next to the butcher shop. That was a happy coincidence for a nine year old boy. I spent many pleasant days in the toy/magic shop. And I had quite the collection of gags and magic tricks including the Wrigley's snapping chewing gum, the King Tut in the tomb magic trick, and the buzz joy. There was also a hamburger grill just down the street on Atlantic Avenue. That hamburger grill was the place where I first discovered my fondness for hamburgers. They got to know me in that grill because I would come in there and I would order three, four, five or six hamburgers. I couldn't get enough of them. Ketchup and pickles – those were my favorite toppings because they always had a barrel of sliced pickles on the table so you could have as many pickles as you wanted; and a chocolate shake. Heaven on earth. We had a White Castle in Atlantic City – one of those hamburger joints with white walls and tiny burgers – but it couldn't hold a candle to the grill near the butcher shop. Next to the grill was a fruit store that sold only the finest fruit, the best of the best. There was no mark on any fruit, ever, and they had a window in front of the fruit shop, although for weeks and weeks and weeks I simply could not tell if there was a window there or not. It was so clean, it was pristine. You couldn't tell if it was a window or just open air. I made a point of walking by the fruit shop just to check out the fruit and see if I could figure out it they were behind a window or not. One day I just had to find out so I reached over just to test it and my fingers hit the window and then I knew there actually was a window, probably the cleanest window on the planet. It was angled so that the light couldn't reflect off it. Clever.

My father was always busy in the butcher shop, sharpening his knives or cutting the meat, talking to the customers. I never saw him at rest. He was a very superstitious man. In the morning when he swept up, he would never sweep out; he would always sweep in and then bring the dust up with the dust pan. It seemed to me an inefficient way to sweep. So I asked him once why he was sweeping in that particular way. My father was a relatively tall man, six-foot-one as he liked to say, well muscled and straight. His face was craggy, but strong, topped by jet black hair which he liked to part and slick back. He had a deep scar – an indent really – on his forehead, to the right, just under his hairline – a reminder of his days in the concentration camps. That scar, he once told me, was the result of a beating he received by one of the hated Kapos. He looked at me with some resignation since I was unaware of the customs of his world. "You always have to sweep in," he said to me, "to bring in the customers. You sweep out, you drive them away." Nothing more need be said.

During the time my father ran the butcher shop my mother worked as well. This was, of course, in addition to maintaining the house. She worked as a seamstress in a factory on Adriatic Avenue. The factory had a government contract to make uniforms for the military. I visited her a few times in the factory. It was large and old, dark and dingy. Hundreds of women working there, sewing away, sewing machines rattling. My mother's particular job was to sew buttons on uniforms. There were great bins of buttons, thousands and thousands of brass-colored buttons, and she spent her days sewing them in place. She worked in that factory for about a year, then landed another job using her sewing skills.

After she left the factory, she worked in a tailor's shop right on the boardwalk, a much nicer locale. From time to time, I would visit her at her shop. It was upstairs on the second floor, traversing an outdoor staircase. It wasn't dingy like the factory. The tailor's shop actually had a big picture window with a nice view of the ocean. The picture window seemed incongruous with the cluttered and noisy tailor's shop. But I doubt my mother spent much time looking out the window. When I visited her at the tailor's shop I would stop by after school and check in with her. My mother would proudly introduce me to the other ladies sewing away in the shop and then ask me to wait for her while she finished up. "Finishing up" usually took an hour or two, but I didn't mind. I would wait for her on the beach, under the boardwalk. It was a great place to play. There was sand under the boardwalk, and the boardwalk itself was 8 or 10 feet above, like the roof of a cave.

The sand on the beach was always hot, but the sand under the boardwalk was always cool, the boardwalk provided shade from the hot sun of the day, and the tiny openings between the boards allowed just enough light to trickle through – in a pattern of light and shade – that a boy could lose all track of time.

"David," she would shout, "David, where are you?" Even though she knew precisely where I was. Or she would whistle to get my attention. My mother developed a special whistle that was meant only for me. It was five notes long, and two notes deep. One high note, one low note, two high notes, one low note. When I heard the whistle I knew it was time to go. It was the Rosenberg family whistle.

Seven

The Boardwalk

You can't talk about Atlantic City without talking about the Boardwalk. That's really what distinguished Atlantic City from every other city on the Atlantic seaboard. That's why people came to Atlantic City. Atlantic City is blessed with very nice weather in the summer and miles and miles of sandy, beautiful beaches. But to stroll along the Atlantic City Boardwalk – to watch the people and be watched in return – that was a tourist's bon bon.

Let me tell you about the boardwalk I knew in the mid-fifties. As I said, Atlantic City was truly a magical place for a kid in those years, and a major part of that magic was the boardwalk. The boardwalk was a wide expanse of wood. There were two lanes in the middle of the boardwalk where the wood ran in a parallel direction to the ocean. All the rest of the boards were placed in a herringbone pattern. Those two center lanes were for the push-carts. In the 1950's there was a combination of actual push-carts – made out of wicker – as well as a few electric carts – always deep blue in color. I imagine the electric carts have now taken over, and the pushcarts are a relic of the past. But in the 50's, the pushcarts prevailed. You paid your money and you could sit back and enjoy the ride. The carts were made for two customers. A pushman would propel the cart along the boardwalk. It was a very civilized and genteel way of enjoying the boardwalk. The pushcarts date back to the 1800's when the privileged wealthy, protected from the sun by parasols, would traverse the boardwalk.

In any event, in the mid-fifties the boardwalk was always packed with people, being pushed along, or strolling along or – on Sunday – riding their bicycles. On Sunday mornings, and only on Sunday mornings, the boardwalk was open to bikes. And lots of people took advantage of that. So did my father and I. In retrospect, it was one of the few things my father and I did together. Sunday morning we would break out our bikes, wrap up against the wind and weather, and head out to the boardwalk. It was a relatively empty place on Sunday morning – very few folks walked it at that time of day, and all the shops were closed. My father and I would get on our bikes and ride on the boardwalk for miles and miles.

I spent a lot of time on that boardwalk. The Steel Pier was in its heyday, and it was my personal favorite. While the Steel Pier was the longest, best known, and most prominent, several other piers stretched out into the sea. The Million Dollar Pier was, perhaps, the next most prominent of the piers. It was short and stubby and was dedicated to amusement rides, pinball machines and games of all kinds. I liked it but rarely visited the Million Dollar Pier as it was pretty expensive – geared more for the tourists and their kids than for a local kid.

The Steel Pier was simply a phenomenal place. Of course, there was an admission price but it was fairly reasonable. And once you paid the admission, you were in and could enjoy the length of it with hardly any other charges. I imagined that I was on a fancy cruise ship in the middle of the ocean. That really wasn't hard to do. Walking along the pier you were actually in the ocean, surrounded by the constantly moving water. The only land was behind you, and so if you didn't turn around you could easily imagine yourself on big ship smack in the middle of the ocean. And the pier itself held reclining chairs, much like a fancy ocean liner.

A major feature of the Steel Pier was Ripley's Believe-it-or-Not. I could, and did, spend hours in Ripley's admiring the fakir reclining on nails that were six inches long, the boy from South America with the hairy face, and the three-headed goat from Kansas. I spent a fair amount of time contemplating which of the three heads might have controlled the four hooves. There was the diving bell, where you could pay a quarter and actually go under the water for a few feet. Cool and quiet. But you could immediately feel the water pressure. There were rides and amusements. But even Ripley's and the diving bell paled in significance next to the Famous Diving Horse of Steel Pier. The dive lasted less than five seconds – but the barker's build-up was terrific. Perhaps they should have called it the Famous Diving Horse's Barker of Steel Pier. The famous diving horse was snow white and powerful, and he would edge himself along to the very precipice of the pier before diving straight into the salty water. He plunged into the brine with a great splash, and then emerged to raucous cheers and applause, before paddling, doggie style to the ramp and steps that took him home. That was the big show.

I had my first date on the Steel Pier. I was ten. Of course I was asked out by the girl. Ten-year-old boys didn't ask girls out on dates. At that age group, girls were always taller, smarter, and more aware than boys. So the girl and I, whose name is lost in the miasma of time, went on a date. She apparently had come into two free admission passes to the Steel Pier and I was the lucky boy to get one of those passes. Her hair was dark and she wore a print dress and carried a purse. I had never seen a girl carry a purse before and I was very impressed. It looked mighty mature to me. I was mildly embarrassed by the fact that she had the passes, but had no clue why I should be. We had a great time. And I believe she gave me a kiss at the end of our day. But I can't be sure because 10-year-old boys can't remember such things.

In addition to the piers, the boardwalk was lined, almost wall-to-wall, with little shops of one kind or another. One after another, non-stop, there was no break to the retail esplanade. There was a plethora of tiny food stands offering every imaginable fast food fair: burgers, hot dogs, pretzels, sandwiches, fries. My favorites were the pizza and the coconut milk. There were penny arcades where literally you could play pinball machines and other machines for a penny. The fancier, more expensive ones were five cents. With a handful of coins (which I managed to extricate from the cash register at my dad's butcher shop) I could spend happy hours in the penny arcades along the boardwalk. I loved the pinball machines but I also had a good time on a mechanically operated baseball game, a real throwback to the pinball machines of the early 20th Century. The player was the batter, and a mechanical pitcher would hurl a metal ball at my mighty bat. If my timing was right, I could smack that ball to the back of the machine where a line-up of slots told you if you were out, or if you got a single, a double, a triple, or the coveted home run.

An assortment of stores lined the boardwalk. Most of them catered to the tourist crowd and offered postcards, sea shells, hardened starfish, sand in a bottle, sun dresses, purses, hats and parasols, beach blankets, buckets and small shovels for the kids. I remember an Aunt Jemima donut and pancake house on the boardwalk which had a donut-making machine right in the window. Now there is hardly anything more fascinating for a boy of ten than a piece of machinery. And I would have to say that a donut-making machine is at the top of the machinery food chain. I could stand outside that window and literally watch that donut-making machine for an hour. It was like a miniature car wash – except without the water – and it was all in a window. The batter would go in one end and some fancy equipment would crank out a donut with the world's most perfect hole. The raw donut would plop into a little lake of bubbling oil and gently float -browning all the way – over to the other end where mechanical arms would flip it and then pull it and all its doughy brothers out, hot and soft on the inside, crunchy on the outside. You didn't even need a topping. You didn't need chocolate or icing or anything; those donuts were perfect just the way they were.

We didn't really do much together as a family. Seemed like my mother and father were always busy working, making enough money to pay the rent and buy the food. But the boardwalk was available and provided relatively cheap family entertainment. So, from time to time when the weather suited, all three of us, as a family, would take an evening walk on the boardwalk. We would join the other families on the boardwalk, strolling, eating and observing. It was a ritual. We would always stop and have a slice of hot cheese pizza. Nobody ever bought an entire pie – it was pizza by the slice. And the slices were always generous. We would wash that pizza down with a refreshing cold cup of coconut milk, delicious stuff, mostly milk but with a taste of coconut. And each of us would always get a scoop of ice cream. This is where I discovered my all-time favorite ice cream, still my favorite, pistachio. And those were the days when you didn't have 63 flavors. Maybe if you were lucky you had five or six flavors, but my good fortune was pistachio was one of them. I passed on vanilla and chocolate and strawberry. But that green ice cream with the little chunks of nut and the slightly sweet, slightly salty taste of pistachio was the perfect way to end a three-course meal of pizza, coconut milk and ice cream. In those days, no one cared about blood pressure or sugar or calories or trans-fats or cholesterol. The focus was on pizza, coconut milk and pistachio ice cream and the memory stays with me to this day.

Just being on the boardwalk watching the people was a great pastime. People in Atlantic City came in all shapes and sizes and in all colors. You had wealthy people, you had middle class, and you had those who just got by. They came to walk on the board-walk and they came to swim in the ocean. No charge for that.

When I wasn't on the boardwalk, I was on the beach. I spent a lot of time on the beach, either in the ocean or playing in the sand. I remember building these huge cones of slightly wet sand and making a little spiral runway for a ball that would start from the top of the cone and roll around the sides and into various holes at the bottom, sort of like a sand pinball machine. I would charge the kids a Popsicle stick to play my sand pinball machine. For some reason they paid up and at the end of the day I accumulated a lot of Popsicle sticks which I intertwined into little rafts, which I either played with or sold for cash money. So I guess in the fourth grade I had become a bit of an entrepreneur on the sands of Atlantic City.

We had real East-coast weather in Atlantic City. Not wimpy seasons like California where the summers were in the 90's and the winters were in the 60's. We had hot and humid summers, we had heavy winds and rains in the fall, and we had cold, ice and snow in the winters. I experienced my first heavy weather in Atlantic City. We had hurricanes every year – some pretty serious – and I remember fear and trepidation as a kid in Atlantic City, in the apartment as that hurricane beat against the sides of the apartment windows and doors. The screen doors would get agitated by the wind and were often banging against the frames. It was a scary feeling living through a hurricane, but of course we lived through it.

The winters were good in Atlantic City – at least from a child's perspective. Nothing like a fresh snowfall on the streets of Atlantic City, making snowballs, forming teams, making snow forts and holding off the neighborhood kids. And of course the summers were great, always warm and wonderful. You could swim in the ocean. The water temperature in the ocean was uniformly mild. And when you got out of the water you could warm up on the beach.

I taught myself to fish in Atlantic City. Trial and error. And the occasional kindness of an adult fisherman who helped me understand the right bait to use (shrimp worked best), the correct weight on the sinker so the baited hook wouldn't be too low or too high in the water, the correct casting technique. I fished from the boardwalk (in those places where it fronted the ocean, I fished from the piers, and I fished from the rock jetties, getting distracted from time to time by explorations into the briny crevices and the discovery of small crabs scrabbling between the rocks. I had a lot of fun as a fisherman. And I actually caught fish. I don't know for sure what it is I caught. They were, indeed, fish. That was good enough for me. I guess they were little sea bass, but I caught them. Some were only 4 inches long, and the "big ones" spanned all of 6 inches. I brought them home and my mother would fry them up in butter for me. They tasted pretty good.

I had my first seafood as a kid in Atlantic City. My mother, my father, and I, discovered – much to our surprise – that we really liked fried shrimp. And once we had our first taste of fried shrimp, we just couldn't stop. It was our absolute favorite meal. There were two famous places in Atlantic City in those days, one called Starn's and the other called Hackney's – both featuring seafood and fried shrimp, both on the beach in Atlantic City. We never could figure out which one we liked better and we kept trying them both. They were both wonderful. Fried shrimp, French fried potatoes –slightly crunchy and golden – coleslaw, ketchup; it didn't get any better than that. Almost every Sunday, like church, we made our trek to Starn's or Hackney's and – never varying the menu – ate our fill of fried shrimp until our stomachs bulged, and debated which of the two restaurants made the better shrimp. I wonder if Starn's and Hackney's are still there today.

My mother in her sun dress and me with my captain's hat in a photo studio along the Atlantic City Boardwalk. You know it's a studio because you can see the radiator next to the plastic horse. I don't know the exact year this photo was taken, but I believe it was the mid-1950's.

Eight

Visiting Mr. Peanut

When we moved to Atlantic City, I was about to start the fourth grade. It was 1955. We stayed in Atlantic City until the start of my seventh grade, which I'll get to in a moment. My fourth, fifth and sixth grades were spent at a school on the southeast corner of Atlantic and Massachusetts Avenues. It was called, fittingly enough, Massachusetts Avenue School. The school was a typical inner-city school, all in one, three-story, brick building. I walked a lot in those days. Walked to school and walked home. Walked up and down the stairs at school, learning to always stay on the right. Still stay to the right to this day. I spent many happy days at Massachusetts Avenue School in the fourth, fifth and sixth grades.

I have a small certificate from Massachusetts Avenue School, to this day. It attests to the fact that I was a member of the Flag Patrol. Every morning, bright and early, before anyone else came to school, I was there to put the flag up the flagpole, and every day after school I would take it down. I rise early to this day. Perhaps influenced by my stint on the Flag Patrol. But that was only the beginning. At Massachusetts Avenue School, the ultimate achievement was to be a member of the Safety Patrol. The benefit of membership in the Safety Patrol was that you got to wear a nifty white belt with a matching shoulder strap that went over the shoulder and then diagonally across the chest to the belt. But the penultimate part of being on the Safety Patrol is that you got a badge that you would affix to the diagonal white strap, and in blue, slightly raised letters it would declare that you were a member of the Safety Patrol and that other students better listen when you told them to cross or not to cross a street. That, to an elementary school student was true power. So I strove to become a member of the Safety Patrol and I achieved my goal. Issued the coveted white belt, shoulder strap and badge, I assumed my post on the corner of Massachusetts and Pacific Avenues and kept a watchful eye out to protect my charges as they crossed that busy intersection. I was very conscientious and soon moved up the Safety Patrol ladder to the office of Lieutenant. Now, the Safety Patrol at Massachusetts Avenue School had three Lieutenants – one in charge of all the Patrol Officers on Atlantic Avenue, one in charge of the Patrol Officers on Pacific Avenue, and one in charge of the Patrol Officers on Mediterranean Avenue. Since Mediterranean Avenue was located furthest from the school, it was our own little Siberia. Lieutenants got the same equipment and badges as regular Patrol Officers, except Lieutenant's badges were embossed with red letters. There was also one Captain, in charge of all the Lieutenants, whose badge was embossed in green letters. As a Lieutenant I didn't have to watch a corner or a crosswalk – I now had the responsibility to watch over an entire group of Patrol Officers and make sure that they did their jobs. I was actually a pretty good Lieutenant and took my job very seriously, but my tenure was short-lived. One day, while performing my supervisory function, one of my charges saw a cat climb into the well of a parked car's wheel. Realizing that this was quick and sudden death for the feline if the car were to start and roll, I summoned two of my Patrol Officers in an attempt to encourage the cat's emergence. Well, we got the cat out, but not before the Safety Patrol Captain had cited me for abandoning my post. And so my career ended, and I had to turn in my badge. If I had had a sword I am sure they would have broken it, and had I had epaulets, they would have been ripped from my shoulders. So, early on, I learned the lesson of setting priorities. I should have let the cat fend for itself, and not gotten distracted from my duty.

I had a friend who lived just around the corner, half a city block from Massachusetts Avenue School. My friend's name was Tad Stern. I spent a lot of time with Tad. We used to play ice hockey in the streets. He lived on a little cul-de-sac, a small L-shaped street, tucked away from the main streets, but very close to school. In the winter his street, which was actually cobblestones, would freeze over and we played some great hockey games on that street, slipping and sliding and shooting a puck. Didn't have ice skates, but we did it in our sneakers. Got pretty cold, but we had a lot of fun.

Tad lived in a three-story house. His grandfather – who was quite old and spoke an unintelligible language – lived on the ground floor. I suspect that the house belonged to him. Tad and his family lived on the second story. I remember his father had a huge model train set, complete with bridges, miniature houses, trees, and people all set up in a special room of the house. Every now and then he would permit us to see it. What a great setup!

At the corner of Tad's street stood a small candy shop, supported primarily by the students from Massachusetts Avenue School, I imagine. I visited that candy shop as often as I had a few pennies in my pocket. My favorite candies were the candy dots on rolls of paper. They were multi-colored dots, but they all tasted the same, hard and sugary. You paid by the inch, but it was cheap. You could get a lot of candy dots for a few cents. You had to bite them off and you inevitably got a little paper with each bite, but it was OK. I also loved the bubble-gum cards. The bubble-gum was flat, sweet and powdery, but was really an after-thought. These were baseball cards, and we bought the packs not for the gum, but for the cards. We would save the cards and we would trade them, but mostly we would flip them, kid gambling as it were. We would flip almost anything, but mostly pennies or bubble-gum cards. One kid would sail his coin or his card against a wall, and then the next kid would do the same. The coin or card that got closest to the wall was the winner and would take the other kid's coin or card. Simple game, and we played it all the time.

I have lost touch with Tad, of course. I have no idea where he wound up.

Years later I went back to Atlantic City, to see what it was like and how it had changed. It had changed. For the worse. It had become a series of slums and devastated blocks in "redevelopment". Every now and then a fancy casino would squat, and the rest of it was bombed out streets and torn down avenues and slums.

Massachusetts Avenue School was pretty much gone. Just a

shell of a building. It looked like it had been hit by a bomb and perhaps it had been. The entire block where my apartment stood was gone, like it had never existed. The boardwalk was just a dim, dim memory of what it used to be.

I can remember when I first moved to Atlantic City, the grand opening of a Planter's Peanut store on the boardwalk. It was bright and new and shiny. The store was full of every variety of peanut, and other nuts as well. But most of all I remember that they had their own Mr. Peanut, a life-size Mr. Peanut statue in front, freshly painted yellow with a snappy black top hat and a brand new cane. But years later, when I went back to visit Atlantic City, I actually found the place where the Planter's Peanuts store used to be. It was empty. Shut down. As I looked through the dirty window, I could see – dimly – Mr. Peanut in the back of the store. He wasn't shiny anymore. He looked pretty shabby. His cane was broken, he was dirty, there were chips in his top hat. To me, the demise of Mr. Peanut was allegorical for what had happened to Atlantic City.

Nine

The Oldest Kid in the Yeshiva

When I wasn't on the boardwalk or beach or in my Dad's butcher shop or mother's tailor shop, I used to enjoy playing in the streets in Atlantic City with the other neighborhood kids. We formed kind of a gang. I got my first leather jacket in Atlantic City. It was the real deal. It was a motorcycle black leather jacket with all the silver zippers and buckles. I had a little captain's hat that I wore, just like Marlon Brando. I would wear that jacket and hat when I rode my bike. I felt real proud of that jacket, felt real proud of being in a group. I wanted to show off the jacket and maybe that's the attraction of belonging to a gang. In any event, we hung out. We had a corner luncheonette where we gathered. We used to go in there to play the pinball machine. There was only one pinball machine in the joint and we played it all the time. We'd get a hamburger every now and then, even though the burgers smelled like fish. But it was our hang-out so it was OK. We'd go down to the beach from time to time because there was an old concrete basketball court there, with metal chains around the hoop instead of a net. We played pick-up games of basketball and it was all right because none of us were very good at it. There was also an old deserted and decrepit foundation shell of a building near the beach. It had high walls, so it became the perfect fort. We used to play in that fort, letting our imaginations run wild. Cowboys and Indians one day, soldiers the next.

I opened my first bank account in Atlantic City. It had five dollars. It took me a long time to save it up. I walked down to the bank and opened an account. They gave me a shiny new pass book. I was very proud of that pass book. Once a month I would go in there and they would update my pass book and show me the interest I had earned. Two cents here, three cents there. And then one day I had accumulated another five dollars for the account, and so now I had more than ten dollars in that account, counting the interest. I kept that passbook in a safe place and would go to the bank regularly to get an update on my interest.

As I walked up Atlantic Avenue toward the bank, the neighborhoods got wealthier and wealthier. I lived at the poor end of Atlantic Avenue, about two blocks from its starting point. If you walked up twenty blocks – toward New York Avenue, Kentucky Avenue, and Indiana Avenue – the streets on Atlantic Avenue got nice looking – some trees, better-looking apartment buildings and nicer looking shops – and as I said, wealthier. I used to enjoy walking on those streets just to see the fancy homes and the fancy shops.

I enjoyed going to the movies in Atlantic City. Movies were only a quarter and so there wasn't a week that didn't go by that I didn't go to the movies with friends. Or if friends weren't available, alone. I never had a problem going by myself.

The schools in Atlantic City were integrated but only partially. In elementary school I had very little contact with black children and I remember being a little bit afraid of black children because of that lack of contact and lack of understanding. There was even a time I was afraid to shake the hand of a black child because I thought somehow the blackness would rub off on me. Foolish thoughts of a child but those were the thoughts I had listening to the comments of my parents. My parents weren't overt racists, but they were certainly not enlightened either. Like most poor white folks, they tended to look down on the blacks. My parents called them "Schwarze" meaning "black people" in Yiddish.

In any event, when it was time for me to go to junior high school, in the seventh grade my parents wanted me to go to Chelsea Junior High School which was mostly white as opposed to Central High School which was mostly black. I never really found out how things got resolved because we moved before I started the seventh grade.

There was a point in time when I was ten years old that my parents decided to send me to the Yeshiva. Now the Yeshiva is a special school set up to teach Jewish children what it is to be Jewish. It's sort of like Sunday school, except it's on Saturday. And it's all about Judaism. It's pretty intense and you have to learn a different language which bears no relationship whatsoever to English: You have to learn Hebrew. My parents had never been very religious. I suppose having lived through what they lived through in the World War and seeing their parents and siblings killed they probably lost most, if not all, of their religion. However, there came a point in time I guess when my parents felt guilty and decided to send me to the Yeshiva to learn what it is to be a Jew.

The problem with that, however, is that most kids start going to the Yeshiva when they are five years old. So here I was, a ten year old, signed up for the Yeshiva, going to classes with the five year olds. That didn't work out too well. I was twice as tall as the rest of the kids, and I felt positively foolish. It was humiliating. I lasted in the Yeshiva perhaps three days; I think I learned the first three letters of the Hebrew alphabet and then I prevailed upon my parents to take me out. I don't think there are many ten year olds that want to go to school with five year olds, so that was the extent of my Jewish education. Of course, that affected the rest of my life because never really going to synagogue, never having the Jewish education, never gaining the understanding of the rituals of being a Jew I never really participated in the Jewish faith for the rest of my life. And ultimately when I turned 60 I decided that I was a Deist, but that's another story for another chapter. I was born a Jew, my heritage is Jewish, but my belief system is that of a Deist. The religion, if you will, of George Washington and Thomas Jefferson, and John Locke and probably Ben Franklin.

If you have ever played the game of Monopoly, you know something about Atlantic City. It's full of houses and hotels of course, its got avenues and areas that you have heard about. Park Place, Marvin Gardens, Atlantic Avenue, and so on. Public transportation being what it was I could get around Atlantic City and I saw most of these places and most of the sites including the famous Elephant Hotel. There was, maybe still is, a hotel in Atlantic City that is shaped exactly like an elephant. It's got a couple of rooms in it and it's a landmark, I guess kind of like the ball of twine that measures ten feet across. The Elephant Hotel is one of the landmarks of Atlantic City along with a somewhat famous lighthouse. But the real landmark of Atlantic City is the Board-walk. Leading up to the Boardwalk are a number of hotels that cater to daily, weekend or long-term stays. I recall going to a Jew-ish hotel with my parents where we would dine from time to time when we weren't eating fried shrimp. I still recall the smell of cantaloupe in that hotel. Just like the Catskills. They say that the sense that brings back the most memories is your sense of smell and I do believe it. Those smells stay with you all your life.

I got my first snorkel diving mask in Atlantic City. I was very proud of that mask. I remember wearing it in the ocean and tread-ing out into the water in Atlantic City up to my waist and then stopping on a funny rock. I looked down into the water through my diving mask at the funny rock because I was going to pick it up and as I looked down with my diving mask I saw that the funny rock was really a hard shell crab with its pinchers reaching for my leg. I think my scream was probably heard in Ventnor or Marvin Gardens. I dashed out of the water in record time and was a lot more careful of what I stepped on when I went out into the water.

Somewhere between the ages of 10 and 11, my mother walked with me to the optometrist to fit me for glasses. I was small for my age, and skinny, not too coordinated actually. The glasses made me look intellectual. Walking out of the optometrist's shop with my shiny new glasses, I noticed that the sidewalk appeared much closer and I felt even shorter. But I could see like a hawk. I've worn glasses every day since that time. No one would recognize me without them.

My father was not what you would call a very warm man. He kept his feelings and his emotions to himself. He was a man of the Old Country. And he had his superstitions. Many is the time we would drive by a person who was deformed or in a wheel chair and my father would roll his eyes searching for metal. He would grab the metal with both hands, spit three times and yell "Hoiker" which, in Yiddish, means "hunchback." My father believed that if he didn't grab metal, spit three times and yell "Hoiker", he or his children would be afflicted in the same way. And if we ever drove by a dog trying to do his or her duty on the side of the road, my father would insist on intertwining his little finger with mine and he would chortle merrily as we went on our way, convinced that so long as our little fingers were entwined, that particular dog could not succeed in its mission.

My father's butcher shop was long and narrow, but well lit and surprisingly cheerful. There was a walk-in meat locker in the back. All in all an interesting place for a kid to go on those hot summer days. We didn't have air conditioning in those days but if you wanted to cool off, a few seconds in the meat locker would surely do it. The interior of the butcher shop was basic white: white tiles, white walls, white ceiling, and white cabinets. The store was dominated by the display cabinets. Behind the display cabinets were the raised wood pallets that my father and his workers would stand on. You had to have raised wood pallets to stand on because when you work with meat there's going to be some blood and some spillage. At the front of the store was a large display window where better cuts were presented, on ice. As you walked into the shop, the counter was dominated by a large ancient cash register. The counter under the cash register was large and open, and contained brown bags of various sizes. Of course, that cave-like area, softened by the brown bags, was the perfect place for me to ensconce myself. In my cave I could see without being seen – every child's delight.

In the middle of the shop stood the butcher block. The butcher block was surrounded by the tools of the butcher's trade: knives of every size and shape, cleavers and saws, all very sharp. When my father wasn't serving a customer, he was sharpening a knife.

There is an advantage to owning a butcher shop. We never lacked for food at home. At the conclusion of the day, my father would bring home food – a chicken, or a cut of beef. My mother would cook it up. My father's favorite meal was brains and eggs. I'm sure that's terribly unhealthy and probably helped lead to his death at the age of 63, but he loved sweetbreads of all kinds, particularly brains and eggs. Chicken, however, was the main staple at our home. My mother could take a chicken and stretch it for many, many meals. Baked chicken, chicken sandwiches, chicken soup, you name it, we ate it all. She also made potato kugel in a large round roasting pan, all ground potatoes and spices and onions, baked in the oven till the outside turned dark brown. She could also make a klops which is a dish made out of hamburger and eggs and bread, sort of like a meatloaf, but like all Jewish food very well baked. Nothing is served rare in Jewish cooking. It's always well done. Jewish cooking is the opposite of sushi.

My mother was a great cook and taught me a lot, probably through culinary osmosis. I still enjoy cooking today; in fact I do the cooking in our household, probably as a result of my mother's teaching. I was, for all intents and purposes, an only child in Atlantic City. My brother, Mitchell, didn't come along till years later. So I was the prodigal son – all attention and focus was on me. My mother doted on me. My father essentially ignored me. Yet, to a great extent, I was on my own. By this time, my schooling had exceeded the education level of my parents. Rarely were they able to help me with my homework or with school projects. So, I had to fend for myself. Sink or swim. I took care of school work as best I could.

Then one day, in 1958, my father announced – out of the blue – that we were going back to Germany. He didn't explain why we were doing this. I assumed in my child's mind that it was a financial decision – that things were – once again – not working out well for my father in his butcher shop. He announced that he would go to Germany first to "set things up" and then my mother and I would follow in a couple of weeks. There was no discussion and no argument. He was a man of the Old Country and he ruled the house. So, if father decided we would move, then we would move. That was it.

So he left. And my mother and I stayed behind. And we were told that when he gave us the call, we were to drop everything and leave everything. Like criminals. We were going to sneak away in the night, so to speak. My father was going to do what in Yiddish is called a "Schtink", which translates loosely to "something smelly." We were to leave the store, leave the apartment, leave the furniture, leave my comic books and Mad Magazines, forget about the bills and take off for Europe. I never really learned why we had to depart in this sudden and ruthless way. I suspect that the bills and debts had exceeded the income that my father was making. I guess this was "Jewish bankruptcy" in action.

And that's precisely what we did. My father left virtually the next day. And soon thereafter, my mother got the call and she and I followed. We carried just a couple of bags of clothing and – in a small cage – the family pet, a parakeet which we had named Budgie (not realizing till years later that naming a parakeet, Budgie is like naming a pet puppy, Dog). Neither my mother nor I had ever flown on a plane before. It was terrifying and exciting all at the same time. I was twelve years old, had no real recollection of my former time in Germany and here we were leaving America, the place to which I had grown so accustomed, to head over to a place where I could not speak the language, a place I didn't know. Munich, Germany, here we come.

Ten

Arriving in Munich

Muenchen (or as it is known in English – Munich) is the capital of Bayern (Bavaria), a large southern state of Germany. Muenchen translates loosely to "home of the monks". It traces its roots back to Catholic monks in the year 750. Today the city is still dominated by Catholicism, and it is a big, metropolitan city – the third largest in Germany after Berlin and Hamburg. In the Middle Ages, because of a bridge built over the Isar River near a settlement of Benedictine monks, Munich became a center of trade and marketing. In 1175, Munich was officially granted the status of a city, and fortifications and walls were built. The city grew and prospered over the centuries and became the hub of Bavaria.

But in 1958 Munich was hardly a metropolis – it was a gray city.

My first trip on an airplane landed me in a strange country, the country of my birth. Germany. It was the fall of 1958 and I was 12. I had just completed a trans-Atlantic flight with my mother and a parakeet. We got off the plane with a few suitcases and made our way, by taxi, to downtown Munich. Everything was very foreign to me. I had just left the only country I had ever really known, America, an affluent, busy, commercial place and had landed in the country of my birth that I really didn't know since I had left Germany at the age of three. There were many remnants and reminders of the war still very visible in Munich. It was 1958 and the war had ended just 13 years earlier. There were many bombed out buildings, there were roads in disrepair, there were no commercial advertisements on the highway. The streets were filled with a multitude of three-wheeled small cars and mopeds. It was all different and unsettling to me – and yet strangely exhilarating.

We made our way to downtown Munich. My father had come

to Munich a few months earlier to set up shop. He had rented a room in a fairly seedy hotel in downtown Munich. The only advantage to it was that it was right in the heart of town, about one block from the main train station. That central location may be why he rented it. It was called Hotel-Haus Muenchen. He had rented us one room, nothing much in it except a couple of beds and a sink and some standup closets. We lived in that little room for a couple of months until my father moved us to another hotel, called the Hotel Ostend (East End), and it was in the Eastern part of Munich, a more modern hotel of about six stories, but typical German construction, very plain, very stolid, very stark.

We lived up on the fifth floor of Hotel Ostend. I don't remember much about that hotel except in the winter we would hang our food out the window in little mesh bags because it was so cold. We used the outdoors as a refrigerator. There was a little kiosk about a half block from our hotel. Munich was full of little kiosks manned by one person, and they would sell everything from newspapers, to ice cream, to candy, to you name it, including milk. I discovered gummy bears at that kiosk and subsequently had many visits to that particular kiosk to purchase gummy bears.

In any event, back to Hotel-Haus Muenchen. It was a fairly simple existence for us, living in that one room hotel. Everything was strange to me, obviously. The people were speaking a foreign language; the signs were all in German. It was, to put it mildly a major life-change for me. I had left everything I was familiar with in Atlantic City, friends, school, everything – without so much as a goodbye – and had come to a foreign country where I knew no one and knew nothing. I couldn't even speak to the people I met but for some reason that intrigued me and never stopped me. From the very first day I ventured out on my own into the streets of Munich, just exploring, smelling the air, the smells of Bratwurst, Schnitzel, and beer, cooking food, and trucks and the sound of street cars, the sound of the city re-building. I emerged from the hotel every single day to just walk around, explore and check it all out.

Within a block of the Hotel-Haus Muenchen there was the Bahnhof, that is the main train station, called Hauptbahnhof,

Haupt meaning main. I spent many, many days just wandering around the Bahnhof. The Bahnhof was the central part of Munich; it had 24 tracks, most of which were filled at any given time with trains coming and going to Vienna, to Belgium, to Luxemburg, to France, just everywhere throughout Germany as well, Berlin, Frankfurt, and Wiesbaden. There were restaurants of all kinds in the Bahnhof selling magazines, food, and candy. There was a theater in the Bahnhof that showed clips running continuously, 10-15 minute clips. I spent many hours in that theater because I discovered that the clips were mostly in English so I would sit there and just absorb and think back to my days in the United States. Some of the bookstores also had tiny sections where they would have five or six or ten books in English. Needless to say I glommed onto those books and spent time looking at them or if I had accumulated enough German marks would purchase them.

I used to enjoy just walking through the Bahnhof listening to the chatter and the sounds, smelling the air and absorbing the sights and sounds and smells of that place. It was gigantic, probably four or five stories high, so high that birds would fly through and it was quite an experience for a young boy of 12.

I also spent time at the department stores. Within one block of the hotel there was a department store called the Kaufhof, which means shopping court. There was another big shopping center called Hertie. These were big department stores and they were fascinating to me. I would walk through the stores floor by floor and just look at the people and the products. German people were very interesting. They love to stare and I was taken aback by this at first, but soon learned to stare right back. I played a little game to see who could out stare who, and after awhile I would win those silly games. I guess they stared at me because it must have been a little odd seeing a 12 year old boy, alone, walking around and through the stores and streets. In Germany, 12 years old is considered a small child, well-protected by parents and grandparents. To see a child on his own, must have been a little disconcerting to their world view.

The department stores were chock full of products. The

clothing seemed old and stogy to me. And it probably was compared to American clothing. There were all sorts of German food and kitchen products, since the Germans love to cook. I would spend a lot of time in the department store section with the spatulas and pans and things of that nature and perhaps this is where I further developed my interest in cooking which served me well throughout my entire life.

Interestingly enough I had no real recollection of Germany when I went back to Germany in 1958. Even though I had been born in Germany, I had left that country when I was under 3. Other than speaking a very few words of German when I left in 1949, the memories of Germany were gone. So it was all new to me. Whatever little German I had known at the age of 3, was long gone, although I learned German later in high school and seemed to have quite an aptitude to pick it up again.

I could, however, understand Yiddish. Yiddish is the language and dialect of the Jewish people and interestingly enough as I learned later on in my life, Yiddish and German are very close. So close in fact that the Bavarian dialect that is spoken in the higher elevations of Bavaria, near where Munich sits, is almost identical to Yiddish.

As a boy I did not speak Yiddish, but I understood it very, very well. So it seems to me that some of the German words did register with me since I did know Yiddish. German, particularly the German spoken in Munich, was very close to the Yiddish language.

German is a land of beer drinkers. Statistically, Germans are among the top three per capita of beer drinking nations on the planet, along with the Czech Republic (then Czechoslovakia) and Ireland. Germans consume beer at every meal and when I walked through the Bahnhof or the department stores, even at breakfast time, people would have beer with their breakfast. It was the obligatory drink when you had lunch or dinner. There was no drinking age in German so even as a young boy if I wanted to have a beer, usually a small one, the restaurants would have no hesitation or compunction in bringing me one. I have only been drunk twice in my life, both of the times on beer. The first time was when I graduated high school, when my friends took me to the Hofbrau Haus in Munich, Germany and I earned my five liter pin. That was quite the experience. Five liters is a prodigious quantity of beer. But I managed to consume it, staggering home on the streetcar. My only recollection of that street car ride home from the Hofbrau Haus is I had to go to the bathroom really, really bad. When I got off the streetcar I remember sleeping twice on the way home on someone's lawn, staggering home and I think I was in bed for two days. That disabused me of drinking for many, many years.

When I first came to Munich in 1958, it was in fact, the beer capital of Germany, if not the world. There were seven great breweries in Munich in those days. They dominated the city, many people were employed by the breweries and beer was the hallmark of Munich. Also the hallmark of Munich was the Oktoberfest, the annual festival, which is actually held in late September on the Theresienwiese, dominated by this huge multi-story statue of a gigantic woman named Bavaria. Tens of thousands, probably hundreds of thousands of people go to the Theresienwiese and the Oktoberfest to gather in enormous tents to drink beer, sing songs, listen to music and carouse. If you go behind the tents you see a line of men urinating in a large trough. Then, they go back in the tents to consume more beer. It is like nothing else on the planet.

Munich is also the home to some of the great art galleries and works of art on the planet. It was a remarkable place for a boy. I would get maps of the city, so I would know how to get around and I would study those maps and the streetcars. You could catch a streetcar in Munich to go anywhere, and the ride was cheap particularly for children. Thirty pfennig and you could ride the streetcar. I would ride those streetcars or walk to the various museums. There was the Deutsches museum, which is one of the world's great technical museums. Great rooms and halls are dedicated to chemistry, physics, biology, the science of music and instruments, astronomy and the like. In the basement of the museum are a coal mine and a salt mine. They are recreations of actual coal mines and salt mines that go on for long stretches. They are quite realistic so you believe you are actually in the coal mine and the salt mine. There are rooms dedicated to ships, rooms dedicated to airplanes, rooms dedicated to metallurgy and the technical sciences. Just a wonderful place for a young boy to hang out and I did. I also hung out at the National Museum, which had some of the great medieval paintings, many suits of armor, axes, swords, maces and the like. There were also displays, miniature displays of castles and forts and Christian themes, all kinds of fascinating miniatures were at this museum. I also liked to go to the Alte Pinothek, which was a great art museum. Some of the works of Rembrandt, Rubens, Duerer and other great artists of Europe were on display. While other kids my age in America were probably watching TV and playing sandlot ball, I was hanging out at the Alte Pinothek and enjoying the works of the great masters.

Munich was also home to the Nymphenburg Palace. This was the palace of Bavarian kings when Bavaria was its own kingdom. It was an intricate palace, very similar to Versailles. The grounds also featured hunting lodges and vast parks. I would hang out at Nymphenburg walking through the baroque rooms looking at the furniture, the paintings, the high ceilings, the chandeliers, the displayed silverware and gold ware and plates and crystal and walk the parks admiring the botanical gardens. Possibly not typical behavior for a 12 year old boy, but it's what I enjoyed and what I found in Munich.

We lived in Hotel-Haus Muenchen for a few months, and then moved into the Hotel Ostend, where we lived for a very long time. I remember going shopping with my mother from the Hotel Ostend to some of the local stores. The local stores were different from what we had in the United States. We had big markets in America, but the local stores in Bavaria in those days were each focused on one product line, so we would go to the store that sold fruit and vegetables and then to the milk store, and then to the bakery and so on. It seemed to me in those days we ate a lot of food out of cans, sardines and herring and meat in cans. And the baked goods, particularly the good German rye bread, couldn't be beat.

I remember the milk store. You would bring your own washed bottles. The shop featured a big pump on the counter and they would pump milk – brought in daily from the local dairies – right into your bottle. That's how it was done in those days.

From the Hotel Ostend, we eventually moved into an apartment on the fifth floor of an apartment building on Augusten Strasse. Augusten Strasse was located pretty close to the heart of town. I could walk from my apartment to the Hauptbahnhof in about 15 minutes. It was also on a streetcar line so my mobility was not impacted in any way, shape or form.

The apartment on Augusten Strasa was very nice and modern, including a small elevator. It was just my mother, father, and me, plus the parakeet – which had lived with us for many years until he was stepped on by a housekeeper one sad day. I had my own bedroom, my parents had their bedroom and we had a nice, although small, kitchen and living room. I could look out the windows at Augusten Strasse and see the hustle and bustle of the street below.

Augusten Strasse was in the part of Munich known as Schwabing, which was sort of the left bank of Munich, the university part of town. Perhaps a mile from where we lived were many cafes and restaurants, places that my mother, father and I would from time to time stroll, get an ice cream cone, and yes pistachio ice cream was still my favorite, and just spend our time watching the folks. I discovered gelato in Munich – including pistachio gelato. But, I was still a student, junior high school student to be exact, a seventh-grader, who had been displaced from Atlantic City, New Jersey to Munich, Bavaria, Germany and I needed to go back to school. The big question was where. I frankly was very nervous about going to a German school since I didn't know any German it would be a very difficult time for me. So I prevailed upon my parents to try to get me into the American school.

Eleven

Going to School in Munich

Now, the 1950's were a time when Germany was still divided, and the Cold War between east and west was in full flower. There was the American zone, the British zone, the French zone and the Russian zone, which became known as East Germany, or the Democratic Republic of Germany.

We were in the American zone. Bavaria was a major portion of the American zone and there were lots of American troops there with their dependents, spouses and children. The US Army ran a significant number of schools in Germany. In fact, Munich was a major location for Army troops and dependents and there was a school there, a very nice school complex with an elementary school, junior high school and high school all connected. The start of the complex was the elementary school, in the middle was the junior high school, and at the end was the high school. They were connected by remarkably long hallways, but they were all independent parts of the school system.

My mother and I went to the junior high school and met with the principal and we were able to convince him to allow me to attend junior high school. We had to pay a tuition, which my parents told me was a fair amount of money, but we were able to enroll me in the junior high school and so I was able to attend the American school even though my parents were not in the military.

I learned later that this was rather an unusual arrangement. I was probably one of only one percent of all the students in all the schools that were not affiliated with the military or the government in some way. But I was happy just to be able to go to the American school.

The problem for me, however, was that although I went to the American school, I had no access whatsoever to things American

– things that students in the United States take for granted. Kids in school want to "fit in"; they don't want to be perceived as "the other". And I was clearly going to be "the other". I had no access to American clothing, and appropriate clothing is pretty important to junior high school students. I had no access to American shoes; I didn't even have access to American food. So, while other kids were wearing the latest in fashion, American tee shirts, American sneakers, American Levis, I had to scrounge around to find things on the German economy that looked something like American clothing. I couldn't even bring a lunch to school on the ubiquitous wonder bread. American white bread was unheard of in Germany and so my sandwiches were on rye bread.

But, believe me, I was happy to be able to go to the American school.

There was a bus, an army bus that went through Schwabing and picked up the students who happen to live there to take them to the American school. The bus ride was a long one. By the time all the students were picked up it was well over an hour. And the students that were picked up by the Schwabing bus were typically students of government workers such as radio-free Europe, or the US Consulate in Munich, and even a few military students, students of military that were "living on the economy" as it was known.

Most of the military lived in military housing facilities, but a few brave ones lived right on the economy and the students would be picked up along with the rest of us to get to school. If I missed the bus, which was a rare event, but happened, I would have to get to school by planes, trains and automobiles. Specifically, I took a long streetcar ride, transferred once and finally got to school, walked about a mile from the end station, past a cemetery (why must I always be walking past cemeteries) to finally get to the school.

My parents went to Germany for a couple of reasons as I found out in later years. Number one, because they weren't doing very well in the United States, had a lot of debts, business wasn't good so they dropped everything and headed to Germany for a fresh start. But number two they also went there to sue the German government for damages and war reparations. This was a process that took many, many years to finalize. Ultimately my mother received a small pension from Germany which she got every month until the date of her death. The Germans are very efficient. In their typical bureaucracy, they would once a year send her a document called a Certificate of Life which she would have to have duly notarized and mailed back to them, to verify yes indeed, Fay Rosenberg was alive.

My father never did receive any money from the German government. My mother in later years said it was because my father always liked to look his best and he always dressed up, wore rings on his fingers, had his hair neatly combed, wore a tie and an impeccable suit, whenever he went to the doctors and psychologists and so they were never convinced he was damaged or harmed by his experience in the concentration camps. In fact he was, since he died very young at the age of 63, from complications suffered in the war. My mother lived on until she died at the age of 84.

In those years in Germany, while waiting for the German government to sort out my parent's claims, we had to earn a living – so my father did whatever he needed to do to make some money. In the early years his primary occupation was selling coffee, tea and cocoa door to door. Every weekend he and I would go to this tiny warehouse he had rented in a depressed part of town. Warehouse is a bit of a laughable term, it was basically a long, dingy room about 15 feet wide and 30 feet deep that was stocked wall to ceiling with various huge bags of coffee, tea and cocoa. We had a counter top and some equipment. Every weekend we would venture to the warehouse to work. We would measure out and fill colorful bags of coffee, bags of tea, and bags of cocoa. We could carefully insert those bags in colorful metal canisters, and then place the canisters in small suitcases. Each suitcase would hold one bag of coffee, one bag of tea and one bag of cocoa. Some of the suitcases were red and some were blue. It would take us hours to do our job filling the suitcases.

So on the weekend we would fill the suitcases and then we

would fill my father's car. He had an Opal station wagon and during the week he would travel out into the country throughout Bavaria, going door to door, knocking on doors, and selling the little suitcases full of coffee, tea and cocoa. Sometimes when he went to villages close by we would see him in the evenings, but often he had to go far afield and we wouldn't see him for days on end, sometimes not until the next weekend when we would go back to the warehouse and fill the suitcases and do it all over again.

My father would also bring with him various candies, chocolates and the like, for sale door to door. I remember going with him on occasion to the wholesaler where he would buy his chocolates and goodies. That was a great experience for a kid. The candy warehouse was very large and stocked full of assorted candies from all over the world, delicious chocolates made by Lindt, Sarote, Tobler and other great chocolatiers of Europe. My father would shop around to try to get the best deals. He would bargain a little bit and he would always let me get a bar or two of the good chocolate to bring home for myself.

But he wasn't always a door to door salesman. My father, after doing the door to door selling for a couple of years, decided to get into the liquor business and so he opened a bar in Munich, which turned out to be relatively successful, which allowed him to open up a second bar. This second bar ultimately transformed into a nightclub with striptease dancers. The dancers were the main draw in this club, the liquor was secondary. He called the club "Parisian". It was located on a side street, in a kind of dingy neighborhood of Munich. The club had a very nondescript front. You could barely tell there was anything in the building. There was just a little sign saying Parisian and once you entered the door you entered another world; a world of drinks, colored lights and ladies walking around topless. I remember very well being around 14 or 15 years of age and going into Parisian. The ladies there treated me very well, took me under their wings so to speak. It was quite an eyeful for a teenager.

I recall helping the so-called architect who designed and set up the interior of the Parisian when my father remodeled it from bar to club. I worked with him for a summer sawing and painting and fixing it up, getting it ready for its grand opening. I wasn't paid, but I learned to handle a hammer and saw.

All this time while my father worked, my mother became a stay at home mom. I don't really know what she did at home all day except cooking and cleaning and doing the laundry, but there was always food on the table, and good food.

Americans who were with the military or the government had access to American goods. They obtained these American goods through the Post Exchange or as it was known the PX and the big grocery store known as the commissary. I and my parents of course had no access to the PX or to the commissary, but we were Americans and we craved and coveted the American food and the American goods. It was very hard to get into the PX and the commissary. There was a person at the door checking ID cards and so we couldn't get in without an ID card showing that you were in the military, or with the US government, or a dependent. Of course, the Rosenbergs didn't have ID cards. And my father and I were turned away a couple of times. But we soon discovered that they sometimes just ignored children. If my parents were to try to get in they couldn't get in without the ID cards but a child like me could sometimes get in without being checked. I guess children are not only not seen or heard, but also ignored – so I would be called upon by my father from time to time to go to the PX and go to the commissary to go shopping.

This was always a little bit nerve-wracking for me because I never knew if I would be stopped and checked and on a couple of occasions I was and was turned away. I would simply mumble that I must have forgotten my ID card. Once the person at the door let me go in anyway, but usually if they checked they would send me out – a humiliating and embarrassing experience to be sure. Most of the time I got in with no checking.

I would try to time my entrance and walk through casually with another family, just making believe I was part of their family and once I was in I was in. And once I was in I would go shopping.

I would buy deodorant, toothpaste, tee shirts and underwear. I would buy lots and lots of stuff. My father would always give me a wad of money and I would try to spend as much of it as I could. I didn't buy just one deodorant stick, I would buy a dozen. I didn't buy just one tube of toothpaste; I would buy 10 or 20. I always got some strange looks from the checkout folks, but no one ever bothered and I would haul out the bags of booty to my father who was outside in the car waiting for me.

Same with the commissary. I would go shopping and I'd get those bags of white bread and bottles of milk and canned goods like pork and beans, all the other American foods that we craved. I would stock up and check out. Did the check out folks ever wonder why a 13-year-old boy was buying bags and bags of food? Perhaps, but no one ever stopped me. And that's what I did. Getting all those bags of American food was like Christmas and Hanukah all at once. I suspect all my life, as a result of this experience in Munich, I've enjoyed going shopping. Certainly something my wife appreciates today.

There was a small clothing store across the street from Augusten Strasse. One day as I was walking past the store, I noticed in the window two American style shirts. I couldn't believe my eyes. All the shirts sold in the German stores were the stodgy German shirts, usually white in color with funny collars. Had I worn those sorts of shirts to school it would have been clear that I was a German and not an American. But that day I saw these two American shirts in the window of the store. I ran upstairs to the apartment and prevailed upon my mother to give me a hundred marks so that I could go across the street and buy these shirts and in fact I did. I cleaned them out; they had two of them. They were actually made in America. I have no idea how those shirts arrived in that little store on Augusten Strasse in Munich, Germany in the early 1960's but there they were. I bought them. They were plaid shirts with button down collars that you could wear either tucked in or out because the hems were rounded. The buttons went halfway down the front and they were very cool. I wore those shirts a lot for many, many years, right through junior high school and into high school. In fact if my memory serves me correctly, I packed those shirts and brought them with me to college and continued to wear them until they fell apart.

Another thing I could not do was go to the American movie on the base. There was an American movie theater in Perlacher Forst where the school and the military housing were located. It showed the latest movies; you could go in to see a movie for a quarter, but again you needed an ID card, so I was not able to see the movies unless someone took pity on me and bought me a ticket. What we would do from time to time, my mother, father and I would go to the movie theaters and I would be asked to find someone to ask to buy the tickets for us. Again, a slightly humiliating experience, but it was worth it to see a good old American movie, eat some American popcorn and be in that entire milieu. So we would go to the movies, I would find a friendly face, I would give them some cash and ask them to purchase a couple of adult and one child's ticket for us and we would go to the movies. I guess if I ever had any shyness, it was all gone by now.

My junior high school years in Munich were adequate. I was a pretty good student and was just there getting my feet wet. I went through the seventh and the eighth grade in the junior high school facility and couldn't wait to get into the high school. I wasn't particularly active in anything in junior high school, just going to the classes and trying to make the grade, but everything changed when I went to high school.

Twelve

I Discover the World of Politics

I remember attending a rally when I was just about ready to finish eighth grade, a high school rally where students were being elected to various offices. I said to myself, "Dave, that's something you've gotta do." So when I became a freshman in high school in the ninth grade at Munich American High, I decided to run for class treasurer. For some reason, which to this day remains unexplained, I won that election. And so I started my political career in 1960 at the age of 14 as a ninth grader in high school in Munich, Germany. I was the freshman class treasurer. I subsequently became very involved in school politics becoming the sophomore class vice-president, the junior class president, the senior class vice-president and a member of the student council. The only election I ever lost was when I was a senior I ran for student body president and lost a very close election to the star high school fullback, whose name was Craig Kessler. In later years I connected with Craig briefly through Facebook. He and I really had nothing in common and politically we were on opposite ends of the spectrum, but he edged me out for the election for student body president that year, and I took the consolation prize running for vice-president of the senior class. A friend of mine, Jim Meade, had already announced that he was running for senior class president and I didn't want to run against him.

I remember as a junior in high school being voted as "most likely to succeed". Regrettably when I became a senior I was not voted most likely to succeed. But I think I won the contest that year for "best hair", as I had a wonderful duck tail.

I was a real activist in high school government, putting a lot of ideas and meat on the table for our discussions. I was also very active in the high school chorus which was a big deal in at Munich

American High School, ultimately being elected president of the chorus. I was also enthralled with and very active in journalism as a junior, becoming feature editor and then editor-in-chief of the high school paper. I was the first student at Munich High who took two years of journalism – I was very dedicated to the subject. They created a special Journalism II class just for me so I could serve as editor-in-chief as a senior for the second year. I was also a member of the chess club and Hank Struzik and I were the disc jockeys who played music every day at lunch. We had a little hide-out above the cafeteria and there we had set up a sound system and a record player and we would play the latest hits. We had a microphone so we could talk to the kids just like real deejays. Interesting enough Hank Struzik after high school went into radio and television and he does that to this day; has a career as a deejay. I loved the cafeteria because I could get real American food.

High school was everything to me. It was my tie and link to America. I was active in everything. I did everything. I ultimately became a National Honor Society student graduating with honors and on the honor roll. I went on school trips to Garmish, to Tegernsee, to Chiemsee. There were actually army recreation centers at places like Garmish and Chiemsee and a guy like me could get an American hamburger there. It was a dream come true for me to be able to go on these trips. I appreciated every single thing about high school.

As junior class president I got to plan the junior-senior prom which was the big event of the social year in high school. All the teens would get dressed up in rented tuxedos and fancy dresses with corsages and dance the night away. My date was Eva Hajek, a really smart and lovely girl, a little shorter than me which was perfect; whose parents were government employees, not in the military. I even prevailed on my mother to go shopping for a "tux" for me. I picked a lurid, multi-colored and sequined tux jacket – that in retrospect must have been hideous. But I thought it was grand. We had a wonderful time at the prom. I remember organizing it in downtown Munich at the Hotel Bayerischer Hof – the classic old-school hotel luxury hotel in town. We had catered food including oxtail soup and Eva looked wonderful.

I had a girlfriend of sorts in high school and her name was Jeannie – she was blond, small, cute, and had braces. We got along fine and she sometimes let me get to second base which to a high school student was very important.

When I was about 15-16 years of age I remember my parents taking me to visit some distant relatives of theirs who lived in a Bavarian town by the name of Cham. Kopinsky I believe were their names and we drove to Cham and visited these folks. They were Jewish and lived in a modest structure near a lake full of reeds. They had a daughter who was about my age, very dark features, and very mature. I felt that she had designs on me. She made numerous efforts to become intimate with me, all of which I rebuffed in as gentlemanly a way as I could. I remember distinctly hearing a little voice inside my head telling me to be very careful. I had things I had wanted to do in life and I didn't want to get tied down in the Bavarian town of Cham.

During my high school years my family moved from the Augusten Strasse apartment to a house very close to Perlacher Forst. The location was very close to the high school. I could actually walk to the high school in about 15 or 20 minutes. We didn't own the house, we rented, but we had the entire first floor of the house, complete with bathtub that you had to heat by burning wood. But it was a real house, like real people and I felt that I had moved up in the world.

One of the reasons we moved was that my brother Mitchell was born in 1960. It was getting a little too crowded and cramped in the Augusten Strasse home so we moved to this house near Perlacher Forst. I was very close to my brother Mitchell in those years. Because of our age difference, about 14 years apart, I was almost like an uncle to him, and I'm sure it was very traumatic when I left home in 1964 to go to college. Mitchell at that time was only about 3 years old going on 4 and one day I just told him I was going to take the garbage out but really I was going to college. So, on that deception I left Munich and went on to college.

Journalism had become very big in my life and so I determined

I would go to college to become a journalist. I also decided that I wanted to go to college in California. Why, California I cannot tell you except that it seemed exotic and interesting to me. I had never been west of Washington, D.C. in my life and here I was in Munich, Germany on another continent, across an ocean, but I wanted to go halfway around the world to California.

So I went to our public library and pulled all the catalogs of California schools that offered degrees in journalism. There weren't many. I remember applying to four schools and ultimately being accepted to two of them. I was accepted to the University of Southern California (USC) and Cal Poly, then known as California Polytechnic State College. Now known as California Polytechnic State University in San Luis Obispo. I didn't know anything about Cal Poly. But I remember applying there because they were in California, they had a Department of Journalism and they had a five dollar application fee.

So the question was: Should I go to USC in Los Angeles or Cal Poly in San Luis Obispo. Ultimately I decided I would rather go to the small town since I didn't know anyone in California. So I packed two half-empty suitcases, had an airline ticket in my pocket compliments of my parents, a one-way ticket to Los Angeles, California, $200 in my pocket, and telling my brother that I was taking the garbage out, took a taxi, and went to the airport on my adventure.

In 1964, I was off to Cal Poly in California to become a journalist.

Thirteen

Hello, California

I was 17 years old and the year was 1964. I had not set foot in the United States for six years, not since 1958. From 1958 to 1964 I had lived in Munich, Germany. Furthermore, my life in the United States prior to 1958 had been limited to three places, all on the East Coast: New York City, a farm in Southern New Jersey, and Atlantic City. From those three places I hardly ventured – a few summers in the Catskills, one school trip to Philadelphia, and one Cub Scout trip to Washington D.C. The vast United States to the west of New York and New Jersey, to a teenager of 17, was all imaginary – the stuff of books, pictures and maps. But here I was, 17 going on 18, on an airplane (the second airplane trip of my life) flying from Munich Airport to Los Angeles International Airport.

This was heady stuff for me. I was traveling to a strange, alluring and wondrous place – California – with all my worldly possessions – two half-empty suitcases and $200 in American money stuck deep into my pant's pocket – for the adventure and challenge of my life. I had never been west of the District of Columbia. But now I was going to the ultimate Western State – California – to go to college: California Polytechnic State College (or as it is now known, California Polytechnic State University) – Cal Poly as everyone called it – in a small town I had never heard of, San Luis Obispo, somewhere in the middle of that huge state. I had no real conception of "California" – just the mental picture that I had created for myself – sun, cars, beaches, waves, women, movie stars. Yet in a sense it didn't really matter if I were traveling to California or Kansas. The important thing to me is that I was traveling back to the U.S.A.

The flight was long. Transatlantic airplanes in the mid-sixties were prop-jets, reliable but noisy and slow compared to travel today. But that didn't matter to me. I was independent, and free, and turning a page to a new chapter of my life. I didn't know a single soul in California and I had only the vaguest notion of how I would get from the Los Angeles airport to San Luis Obispo and Cal Poly. I knew only three things: I had been accepted to Cal Poly as a first-year student majoring in Journalism, a room in a dorm (Sequoia Hall) had been reserved for me, and the roommate who had been chosen for me by Cal Poly was a first-year electrical engineering student by the name of Emmanuel Harris Hirschbein, born on November 20, 1946. Since my own date of birth was November 20, 1946, I concluded that the convergence of birth dates (and the likely fact that Emmanuel Hirschbein was Jewish) were the prime factors which resulted in our assignment as roommates.

My plan was to arrive at the LA Airport, collect my luggage and flag down a taxi. I would ask the driver to take me to an inexpensive hotel near the bus station. I would rest up at the hotel that first day. Next day my plan was to catch a Greyhound bus to San Luis Obispo. Then another taxi and – voila – I would be at Sequoia Hall. Much later in my life I realized how truly foolish my plan was for a number of reasons. First of all, the taxi ride from the airport to a "hotel near the bus station" was a long one and used up a good one-fourth of my monetary nest-egg. Second, any such "hotel near the bus station" would necessarily be located in the seediest, dirtiest and most dangerous part of Los Angeles. I was not disappointed.

The taxi ride from the airport to the hotel was invigorating. My eyes were glued to the windows of the cab while I inhaled the sights of Los Angeles. I couldn't believe the number of billboards and advertising signs – they seemed to be everywhere! But while the cab ride was a visual stimulant to me, it also cost me a good $50. My funds were depleting and I had barely begun.

The hotel was located only a block or two from the Greyhound Bus Station but it had seen better days, perhaps 50 years earlier. The hotel was old, and not particularly clean. The room was small, spare and creaky. It had a threadbare carpet, but that served me well. I peeled off $40 from my diminishing financial stash and placed the other bills under a corner of that carpet for safe-keeping. I put my $40 into my pocket, put on a jacket and decided to stroll around the downtown near my hotel, and also go to the bus station to find out the bus departure schedule for the next day. I had $40 and a few coins in my pocket, and happy as a clam at low tide, I walked around jingling those coins, breathing in the air, absorbing the sounds, smells and the sights of the city. It was exciting stuff.

I passed a small men's clothing store and saw some shirts in the window. I was a kid in a candy store. They were nifty dress shirts with small holes in the collar where you could slide a bar under your tie. One of them even had a snap-device to hold your tie in place. I had to have those shirts, so I went into the shop and bought three of them. I used up close to $20 of my money, but it was one of the most satisfying purchases of my life. Finally, after six years in Europe, I was able to go into a shop and buy real American clothes.

I made my way past panhandlers and prostitutes to the Greyhound bus station and checked the times and fares. All my life, seemingly, I left little to chance and always had to plan ahead. Armed with the shirts and the bus schedule information, I made my way back to the hotel room. In retrospect, I cannot remember if I ate any dinner in Los Angeles. It probably didn't matter. I was drinking and eating the sights and sounds and I returned to my seedy room, double-locked the door, pulled my money from the carpet, and fell promptly asleep.

The next morning, bright and early, I checked out of "Hotel Seedy." I took my suitcases in hand and walked back to the bus station, boarded for the trip to San Luis Obispo, and off we went. The trip to San Luis Obispo, the home of Cal Poly, took several hours as the bus made many stops. It was not an express bus —actually more of a milk run. But that was all fine with me. I absorbed the sights along the freeway. Even the word "freeway" was new to me. Back East they were "through-ways", "park-ways" and "turnpikes". In Germany they were "Autobahns". But in California, these broad highways were called freeways. And I marveled at the multitude of big American cars (in Europe, big American cars were a rare oddity), the billboards, and the fast food restaurants that we passed along the way. The drive to San Luis Obispo was pleasant. I was aboard a puddle-jumper bus that stopped at several towns – Ventura, Santa Barbara, Santa Maria – along the way. That was perfectly fine with me. Everything I saw was new and inviting. We were driving north on Highway 101, but on occasion we would merge with scenic Highway 1 and I would get my first glimpses of that great ocean – the Pacific. I was familiar with the Atlantic, of course, having lived for years in Atlantic City. But the Atlantic was merely the Pacific's little brother. The Pacific is brawny and tough. I was amazed at the power of the waves and the impact of that ocean on the shoreline, crags and rocks below the highway.

I saw my first surfers on that trip up the Central Coast. Tiny humans with wooden boards tied around their ankles, challenging the waves. Indeed, I had arrived in California.

The trip from the Downtown Los Angeles bus station to the San Luis Obispo bus station lasted close to four hours, and it was mid day when I rolled into the town. San Luis Obispo in 1964 was a sleepy hamlet on the Central California coast, just a few miles from the ocean. The town has two claims to fame. One was the wonderful old Mission San Luis Obispo – one of the original missions of the Spanish padres of California, arches and all – well-preserved and located smack in the center of town. The other is the University – in those days called a College – Cal Poly. The town of San Luis Obispo is unique because it is located almost dead center between two major metropolitan areas: Los Angeles to the south and the San Francisco Bay Area to the north. It was close enough to those areas that the students could visit parents and vice versa, if they wished; yet far enough away that they didn't want to do it every weekend. Further, San Luis Obispo (or "SLO" as we called it) was distant enough from the metropolitan areas of the state that it became quite the self-contained little village. It was impractical to travel to the big city to shop or to seek entertainment venues – so San Luis Obispo residents stayed close to home to do their shopping and entertaining. Plus Pismo Beach offered entrée to the Pacific Ocean, just minutes from San Luis Obispo.

The town of San Luis Obispo is laid out in a grid system, and unlike most California towns which are oriented to the automobile and contain just one long main shopping street, San Luis Obispo actually has a downtown shopping district. The bus pulled into downtown San Luis Obispo. The bus station in SLO was remarkably small in comparison to the LA bus station. Easy to get around. I found one of the two taxis that serviced the town, and I made my way to campus. My destination was Sequoia Hall – the dormitory to which I had been assigned. The cab ride – this time – was thankfully short. The campus is just about 5 minutes from the downtown. Mercifully, the taxi ride was cheap as my financial stock was sinking fast. We drove onto campus and virtually the first image I had of Cal Poly were the brick dormitories, Sequoia Hall being right out front. On a small hill behind the dorms, about half way up, were the letters "Cal Poly" reminiscent of the "Hollywood" sign in the town of that name. Except the letters "Cal Poly" were cement and were flush against the hill. But I thought, as I saw them: Well, here I am at college!

I paid the cabbie and made my way up the steps – ice plant with pretty purple flowers on either side of me – to Sequoia Hall. The dorm was a 3-story structure of red brick, simple, functional and plain. It was set on a rolling hill, the first of five or six identical buildings, all with picturesque names reminiscent of California – Tehama, Muir, and the like. The dorms were built on higher ground, so that once up the steps I had a panoramic view of much of the campus which spread out before me. The campus administration building was directly in front of me. Next in line was the sprawling one-story cafeteria where I was to spend many a happy meal scarfing up those hamburgers and other American foods which I had missed for the past six years. The campus gymnasium was to the left of the cafeteria. Academic buildings were everywhere – education, mechanical engineering, journalism and printing, and more. I gathered in the view, and made a mental picture which has stayed with me to this day. Then I turned, bags in hand, and entered Sequoia Hall.

I have a vague recollection of "checking in" with a resident manager or resident advisor and being assigned a room on the second floor. Each dorm had a resident manager who was the major domo of the dorm – typically a senior – who had a larger than normal room on the first floor. And each of the three floors had a resident advisor who was a junior or senior. Resident advisors got a standard room, but no roommate so they had the room to themselves. There was no elevator in the dorm, so up the steps I went to my designated room. I walked in to find my roommate for the year – Emmanuel Harris Hirschbein – truly a million-dollar name. "Just call me Mannie", he said, and stuck out his hand. We shook hands and were instant buddies.

Mannie was just about my height, perhaps an inch shorter, sturdy, swarthy, with close-cropped hair, the semblance of whiskers, large dark-rimmed glasses. He wore a white T-shirt, jeans, and sneakers – he affected the surfer dude look and attitude, but looked nothing like a surfer. Mannie had a pleasant, if slightly lopsided smile. The important point, however, is that Mannie had a car. We hit it off immediately.

My roommate had already ensconced himself on one side of the room, so I took the other. The room was minimalist even by the standards of a minimalist. The outside brick, I found, was also inside. The room was quite small. It had a door and a window, plus a closet for each of us. The furniture consisted of two beds, two desks, two chairs, two cork boards on the wall, and two metal dressers. There was literally only two or three ways you could arrange your furniture. We arranged the furniture, and would from time to time re-arrange. We decorated the room to our liking.

Mannie was a Southern California boy. Even though he didn't have the blond hair and surfboard, in his mind he was a Beach Boy. We wound up doing almost everything together, and became fast friends. Having a car helped. It was an older model tank of a car – a Ford – and it had a stick shift. I had no driver's license so Mannie was the designated driver every time. And he loved tooling that car around town, and down to Pismo Beach. Mannie was the kind of fellow who believed that his car simply would not run unless he turned the radio on to a rock and roll station. So we drove around, Mannie shifting gears like he was Parnelli Jones, listening to the beat of rock and roll, with Mannie singing refrains from time to time.

The fact that Mannie's mother could cook didn't hurt things either. Every time Mannie returned from a weekend visit to his house, he would bring back a boatload of goodies, which he was more than happy to share. I had no place to go on weekends, so I hung around the dorm with a couple of foreign students who also had no place to go. From time to time, Mannie would take pity on me and I would travel with him to Southern California to visit his parents, inhale their food, pet their full-size poodle Pierre, and then truck back to college. When I visited, I used the guest bed that Pierre usually used – so that dog glared at me a lot. It was the good life.

Cal Poly and the college life was a mélange of sights, smells and sounds for me. I especially loved cafeteria meals – perhaps the only Boy in America who could say that. Everything they served – breakfast to dinner to snacks – was great in my book. I looked forward to Sunday lunches. On that day, at lunch, the cafeteria always served cheese burgers. Unlimited quantities of cheese burgers. What a treat for the kid from Munich.

When I wasn't hanging out at the dorm or glutting myself in the cafeteria, my life on campus was focused on work and class. I was not independently wealthy, so I worked. I believe that over my years at Cal Poly, I held every single job that campus had to offer – all of them paying about $1 per hour. Alternatively, I worked in the dishwashing room at the cafeteria (I actually enjoyed the conveyer belt assembly line set up in the cafeteria – I got pretty good on garbage disposal duty and on glassware), gardening, janitorial work (I loved working in the aeronautical engineering building – everything was so clean and shiny), selling tickets at rodeos and football games, working in the vet hospital (I was quite the expert with the autoclave), and every other odd and end job I could pick up. I would receive an occasional check from the folks back in Munich, but by-and-large, if I wanted money to buy clothes, food off-campus, books, toilet articles, or simply go to the movies, I had to earn that money.

The main focus of my life on campus, however, was my chosen major – Journalism. I loved it. I learned a great deal about the craft at Cal Poly. The philosophy of the Cal Poly campus is "learn by doing" so I got the most practical education possible. It wasn't theoretical – it was a hands on, get it done kind of education. Perfect for me. I took classes in writing, editing, advertising, marketing, even printing. We had a daily paper on campus – the Mustang Messenger – and I worked on that newspaper in every possible capacity. I worked as a reporter, took some photos (but wasn't particularly good at photography), worked as an editor, and even wrote a column called "From the Horse's Mouth" (the campus mascot was the mustang). It was slightly political and slightly humorous (with the emphasis on "slightly") and some whom I offended called it "from" a different part of the horse's anatomy. Journalism had its own building on campus which it shared with the Printing major. We had an entire printing plant in the basement. We even had ancient linotype machines down in that basement. I could watch those machines for an hour – the operator would type out the letters on the keyboard and the machine would cast the letter as he typed in hot lead, speed it into place and cast a line of type. Fascinating stuff. We learned the business from the ground up.

Holidays – like Thanksgiving and Christmas – were especially challenging for me. Everyone took off, heading home – but that was out of the question for me. I stayed on campus. However, I couldn't even stay in Sequoia Hall. They shut it down for the holidays and moved the handful of us that remained to what they laughingly called "The Cardboard Jungle" – a series of ramshackle wooden buildings left over from World War II where the five of us (a few African students and me) stayed. The rooms were spare, the walls were thin, the heater hardly worked and the showers were communal and "down the hall". Plus, I had no transportation

– only a bike. Virtually everything on campus was shut down for the holidays – even the cafeteria. Fortunately, the campus dairy operation remained open (dairy cows had to be milked) so I could visit their outlet store and purchase milk and cheese – and with whatever I could buy from the automat machines, I survived.

But when the students came back after the holidays, life on campus was good. Besides my studies, I promptly signed up for ROTC (the Reserve Officers Training Corps) soon after my enrollment as a Freshman. It was 1964 and America was very divided over the Viet Nam War, but at Cal Poly, ROTC was big. Of course, we had the protestors against the war, but the Cadet Corps far exceeded the number of war opponents – in fact, we had so many members of ROTC that we had an entire Brigade of ROTC cadets, composed of three Battalions. I wasn't very politically sophisticated at this stage of my life, and frankly, didn't really focus on Viet Nam one way or the other. The only thing that mattered to me was that I was determined to become an Officer in the U.S. Army – to me (after my years in Germany as a student) that was a high calling. I was honored to join the Cadet Corps.

I moved up very quickly in rank during my four years in the ROTC program. At the conclusion of my four year stint, I had attained the rank of Cadet Major (I was in the top cadre as we had only one Cadet Colonel, four Cadet Lieutenant Colonels, and only six Cadet Majors). I also joined the Society of Scabbard and Blade, attaining the position of First Sergeant of the Society. When I graduated from Cal Poly in 1968 with a Bachelor of Science Degree in Journalism, I was also commissioned a Second Lieutenant in the U.S. Army, and I was made a Distinguished Military Graduate. As a DMG, I was given my choices of branch and assignment and I took advantage of that opportunity by choosing the Adjutant General's Corps and assignment in Europe.

While at Cal Poly, I decided to dabble in student government. I actually ran for Student Body Vice President, but it was a half-hearted effort. I ran as a write in candidate, and that never really works, but I still came in second place to Amos Ngongi, a student from Africa, who was elected to the office and served without much distinction. But my run for office apparently impressed the Student Body President who negotiated a contract with me to develop and run a student body newsletter. I did so and "Pegasus" was founded. It became a mouthpiece for student government and a counter-point to the Mustang Messenger, and I printed out a few editions, till I lost interest, and went back to the Messenger as Executive Editor. But it was fun while it lasted.

Perhaps my main extracurricular focus at Cal Poly was the fraternity I helped to found. During the years I attended Cal Poly, fraternities were not recognized campus groups, and the few that we had were all located off-campus. Actually, there were only six or seven fraternities, but no "Jewish" fraternity. So a few Jewish men decided that they wanted to form one, and affiliated with Alpha Epsilon Pi, an established old-line National Jewish fraternity. Even though I wasn't an active Jew, I enjoyed taking charge, so I joined the group as well. There were about 12 of us, and we started a fraternity from scratch – we even got a house, furnished it and set up the rules. I was living at the time with Mannie in an apartment we had rented off campus. Mannie joined the fraternity as well, but while I moved into the fraternity house, Mannie decided he would continue to live in an apartment which he then shared with a friend of ours – a printer – Marc Pupkin. I was elected the first Master (President) of the house and I had a great deal of fun getting the fraternity started and established. I guess I was also a bit of a troublemaker since – under my presidency – we admitted Catholics, Protestants, ethnic minorities to our little fraternity. We got some flack from our national – but we continued to do it. The fraternity has continued at Cal Poly to this day.

Dave the college student at age 19

Fourteen

I Meet a Special Lady

I have found that my life is a series of stepping stones, one leading to the next. And setting up the fraternity was another stepping stone in my life because, ultimately, it led me to the most important single event in my life: the meeting with the woman who would ultimately become my wife.

In my third year at Cal Poly, one of my fraternity brothers – Gary Kwart – set me up on a blind date. In fact, it turned out to be a double-blind date. One of my fraternity brothers (and a fellow ROTC member) David Plummer and I were both set up with blind dates. My blind date's name was Lea Pepper, a transfer student from a Junior College. Turned out both David Plummer and I wound up marrying our dates. I lost touch with David over the years, but I understood that he went to Viet Nam as a Second Lieutenant and died there. I think I was charmed with Lea from the first moment that I met her. She was short and sweet, terribly attractive, full of energy and had the biggest, most expressive eyes I had ever seen. Although I didn't know this at the time, after our first date, when I had dropped her off at her dorm, she had a second date waiting for her. I was glad to be part of her social calendar. As it turned out, Lea Pepper cleared her social calendar after that date – just for me.

I was always a decisive fellow and it was no different with Lea. I met Lea in September of 1967. I gave her my fraternity pin in October, asked her to marry me and became engaged to be married in November and we wed the following June – specifically June 30, 1968.

After we met, Lea and I were always together. I would sneak into her dorm – Jesperson – whenever I could. The girls who lived in this all-girl dorm got to know me very well, and they facilitated our illicit dorm time. Lea and I went to dances, concerts, movies, Morro Bay – I visited her folks (Dr. Herman Pepper and Dr. Genevieve Gaard) in Redwood City. My folks had eventually decided to follow me to California, and had moved to Los Angeles, opening up a liquor store. So, from time to time, Lea and I would visit them as well. Soon after we met, Lea and I moved into an apartment together and set up house. Life was terrific. Lea had a friend – Nancy Newman – who was living in Santa Barbara – and we would visit that wonderful beach town and enjoy each other's company.

Lea changed my life, and I guess I changed hers. When she came to the campus as a transfer student from Canada College, she chose a "Home Economics" Major. But as Lea has no homemaker skills whatsoever, and that major emphasizes math and science, it was an unfortunate choice for her. I convinced her to change her major to Journalism and she seemed much happier. We helped each other with our work, and as writing was a breeze for me, I would up writing many of her papers, as well as my own. Lea did the typing.

Our wedding was quite the event. The Drs. Pepper and Gaard made sure of that. We had a Big Wedding in a Big Synagogue. Four bridesmaids, four groomsmen. Judy Pepper – Lea's sister – was the maid of honor, and Mannie was my best man. Herman Pepper's brother, Arthur and his wife Stella, came from Scarsdale, New York for the wedding. Arthur and Herman looked so much alike it was scary. And Stella was the archetypical New York Jewish, mah-jongg playing, cigarette-smoking matron, complete with accent and throaty voice. I must confess that I was in a bit of a daze all day long. However, I have seen the wedding pictures so I know that it happened. We didn't have a great deal of money so we took our Honeymoon in Yellowstone National Park, driving all the way there and all the way back. And we've lived happily ever after.

During my sojourn at Cal Poly, I spent two summers in Chico, California, working as a reporter for the Chico Enterprise-Record. One summer was "pre-Lea" and the other summer was "post-Lea".

I had a grand time in Chico, even though it was hotter than Hades. The town has the second largest park in the US – Bidwell Park – and a long street called the Esplanade, in addition to the traditional Main Street and Market Street that we see in so many California cities. Chico is a college town, but it's also an established community so far away from any other major metropolitan area that it was a force onto itself. And the newspaper was the big show in town. Everyone subscribed to it and read it. I was hired as "summer relief" so I took over for the regular reporters. I did the city beat, the county beat and the police beat on alternate weeks. They even made me "farm editor" for awhile and I had the fun of editing the farm page and getting to know all about Future Farmers. (That knowledge actually served me well back at Cal Poly. One of the jobs I held at Cal Poly was as Editor of the California Future Farmer Magazine – easy work and it paid well.) I loved working on the Enterprise-Record. It was a full-fledged daily paper, with all the trappings of a big city paper, complete with print shop adjacent to the newsroom. Working on a daily paper was instant gratification – every day I saw my name in print over the results of my day's work.

The Enterprise-Record didn't pay very well – $1 per hour – but I could live cheaply in Chico so it was fine. Lunch was less than a buck at the local hamburger joint near the newspaper office. The E-R was the local fiefdom of A.W. Bramwell, who like most newspaper moguls, inherited the paper from a grandfather and thus, was instantly knighted with newspaper savvy. Milan Murray, an ancient soul, tall and thin as a rail, was the Managing Editor, although other than writing editorials, I never really knew what he did in that job. The heart of the paper was Eddie Booth, the city editor. Eddie weighed 400 pounds or more and I never really saw him move from his overstuffed chair. Eddie chain-smoked Camel cigarettes, unfiltered. He went through three or four packs every day. A large white ceramic ashtray always sat in front of him, filled with small gray snakes, the remains of his cigarettes. His desk drawers were neatly stacked with Camel packs. When I came to work in the morning he was there in his regular city editor's spot at the apex of the "U-shaped" city desk. When I left he was still there. In his right hand he held a thick pencil which he used constantly to mark up the copy (which we reporters typed on yellow spools of paper on our manual typewriters). When he finished marking it up and putting a headline on it, a runner would take it over to the adjacent print shop where it would be set in type.

The newsroom was day and the print shop was night. Both were noisy. But the newsroom was open and airy with slick linoleum floors. The print shop was dark. It reeked of oil and sweat, newsprint and ink. That oily-inky stuff hung on everything, including the printers who worked there. It was the special world of print journalism and I loved it. Would have stayed in it as well, but I figured out toward the end of my sojourn in Chico that Journalism – at least in 1968 – didn't pay very well. Plus I was coming to the realization that I would rather make news than just report it.

I did well in College. I graduated with honors in 1968 with a 3.4 GPA. (These were still the days before grade inflation. In 1968 you had to work hard for an A. Today, folks get A's for showing up and not looking bored.) I received a B.S. in Journalism (perhaps the only school in the USA that gives a B.S. for Journalism). At the same time, I received my Commission as a Second Lieutenant in the U.S. Army, and was assigned to the Adjutant General's Corps in Germany. And so, for the third time in my life, I was destined for Germany.

*A card I drew and gave to Lea on our 52nd
wedding anniversary.*

LT. DAVID ROSENBERG'S MOTHER FAYE PINS BARS ON HIS UNIFORM
Admiring new hardware are his wife Lea and Poly president Robert Kennedy.

In 1968 I graduated from Cal Poly and was also commissioned a second lieutenant in the US Army. Here, as Lea watches, my gold lieutenant's bars are pinned on by my mother and Dr. Kennedy, the President of Cal Poly.

Fifteen

You're In the Army Now

Officers in the U.S. Army, at least in 1968, were required to purchase their own uniforms. And so, that's what I did. I purchased a very nice dark green Class A uniform, a couple of light tan Army shirts, black shoes, black socks, black tie, and cap. I had to also purchase all the patches, rank insignia (one gold bar on each shoulder as a Second Lieutenant), gold officer stripes for the pants and sleeves, as well as the Class B fatigues. Had to get them all tailored to fit, including the obligatory pegging of the fatigue pants so they would look sharp tucked into the black combat boots. I must confess I looked good in uniform. I was thin and fit, and the tailored clothes made me look the part of an officer, even though I was the most junior of junior. In 1968 I was 21 years old.

Even officers have to go through basic training, although it is not as demanding or rigorous as the basic training that new enlisted personnel have to endure. So, I was sent to basic training. The location of training is dependent upon the branch to which one is assigned. Infantry officers go to one camp, armor officers go to another, artillery officers go to yet another, and so on. I was assigned to the Adjutant General's Corp and so I was sent to Fort Benjamin Harrison in Indianapolis, Indiana – the traditional home of Adjutant General's Corp Officers and Finance Corps Officers. These were not combat branches and so Ft. Benjamin Harrison acquired the nickname of "Uncle Ben's Rest Home." Even though basic training at Uncle Ben's wasn't viewed as rigorous by the standards of Infantry, Armor and Artillery, it was nevertheless typical Army training. We lived in large dorms, shared communal bathrooms, got up before the sun was up, did calisthenics, ran miles each day, learned to shoot weapons of all kinds, ran obstacle courses, crawled under barbed wire, and ate at the mess hall. In fact, I surprised myself on how well I did. I remember running the mile in under 8 minutes while in full fatigue uniform including combat boots, I qualified as an expert in the rifle (even though I had never fired a weapon prior to basic training), and I had a great deal of fun firing the M-79 grenade launcher (it made a very satisfying "pop" sound when launched and the grenade moved so slowly, one could see it in flight for the entire arc).

Since I was newly married, my wife, Lea, was able to accompany me to Indianapolis. We rented a small, but comfortable apartment near the base, and Lea and I could see each other on the weekends. It was winter in Indiana and cold. Poor Lea, packed in sweaters, coats and furs, slipped on the ice one morning, and took a hard fall. But the layers of clothing pretty much protected her, and the only damage was to her dignity. Otherwise, life was pleasant enough for my new bride and me. We got through basic training fairly intact. My commitment to the Army, as an officer, was six years: two years on active military duty, three years in the Ready Reserve, and then one year in the inactive Reserve. Basic training was part of my two-year active duty commitment. And as basic training wound up, Lea and I looked forward to the next big step in my Army "career" – my duty assignment.

In 1968, the war in Viet Nam was ratcheting up dramatically and the Army was filling its enlisted ranks through the draft. The Army had many branches in those days. I have already mentioned several of them (Infantry, Armor, Artillery, Finance, Adjutant General's Corp) such as Engineer, Signal, Ordnance, Quartermaster, Transportation, Chemical, Medical Services, and others. The largest branches, of course, were the so-called combat branches of Infantry, Armor, Artillery, Engineer and Signal. The smallest branches included Finance and Chemical. And the smallest branch of all was the Adjutant General's Corp to which I had been assigned. The Adjutant General's Corp is one of the oldest branches of the Army, going all the way back the General Washington's Day and the Revolutionary War. The branch is under the jurisdiction of The Adjutant General – a Major General working at the Pentagon in Washington, D.C. In 1968 the branch had four functions in the Army: it handled the administrative paperwork of the Army, it handled the personnel work of the Army, it ran the military post offices, and it ran special services for the Army. Special services is the Army's euphemism for "recreation" and the Special Services Officers were in charge of all the recreational activities for the troops (and dependents) in their respective jurisdictions. "Recreation" was a broad term which could include movie theaters, libraries, bowling alleys, service clubs, entertainment centers, craft shops, auto shops, gymnasiums and sports facilities, teen clubs, USO touring shows, tours offices, recreation facilities, and the like. In fact, of the four functions, special services was the smallest unit. My dream, and hope, was to be a Special Services Officer. I surmised that this function was in my wheelhouse, and I would be well-suited to perform those duties.

So, it was a little disconcerting when I learned that I had been assigned to be a Postal Officer for the U.S. Army. In my training, I had learned that being a Postal Officer was a very important function in the Army – but to me it sounded infinitely boring. Plus, a Postal Officer has to be responsible for every penny and every stamp that crosses his or her desk. If there is a shortfall, the Postal Officer has to fix it, out of his or her own pocket if necessary. But, if the Army orders it, you gotta do it. So, off I went to prepare myself to be a Postal Officer in Germany.

The training to be a Postal Officer was unremarkable. In fact, I would call it ludicrous. My training consisted of one day in the United States Postal Annex in New York City. The place was gigantic, filled with people and mail. My training consisted of being put in a small vehicle and being driven, for most of the day, through the Postal Annex and all its cubbyholes. Now, fully "trained" I was ready to assume my duties.

My orders came through, assigning me to Support District Hessen, in Frankfurt, Germany. Before I could hop on a plane, however, I had a brief diversion in Scarsdale, New York. Turns out that I had caught a case of pneumonia while going through basic training at Fort Benjamin Harrison. The pneumonia knocked me for a loop and it took about two weeks to recover. Lea and I stayed with her relatives in Scarsdale, New York, and I went to the local hospital every day for "inhalation therapy". It worked, and fully recovered, I made arrangements to fly on a military transport plane to Frankfurt, Germany, located in the middle of the German State of Hessen. Germany, at the time, was still divided into West Germany and the communist sister, East Germany. Tensions with the Soviet Union would wax and wane, particularly during the days of the Viet Nam war.

Lea and I had determined that Lea would accompany me to Germany. It was a big adventure for us. The plan was that I would travel to Germany first (shades of my father), get established, arrange for a place to live, and then Lea would soon follow. So, following this plan, I caught the transport to Frankfurt, and after a long and unremarkable flight, I arrived in this industrial and commercial center of a burgeoning Germany – ready to assume duties as a Postal Officer.

Well, that never happened.

I had barely stepped off the plane when a young officer by the name of Captain Hamilton spotted me, bee-lined over to me, asked me my name, and asked to see my orders. When he saw that I had been assigned to Support District Hessen, a broad smile crossed his face, he shook my hand, and said, "Welcome to Germany, Lieutenant, you are going to be assigned to Army Support Services, as the Deputy Support Services Officer." Of course, I had no idea what he was talking about, and I had never heard of Army Support Services, but he was a captain and I was a lieutenant and I was not about to argue with him. Captain Hamilton took me in tow and drove me to his office. Turned out his office was a two-story building near the center of Frankfurt on a pleasant tree-lined street. He showed me around. And I learned that Army Support Services is, essentially, the Army's welfare and social services office. Virtually all lower-ranking enlisted personnel in the Army (privates, specialists and corporals) would be on welfare if they were civilians – the pay was pretty meager. And many of them had wives and children to support. So, Captain Hamilton was the man in charge of helping these soldiers with their needs of daily life – food, clothing, furniture, housing, etc. It was a huge and important task, and he was determined that I would be his deputy. The reality of the situation was that the Army was dramatically understaffed everywhere except in Viet Nam. Officers were few and far between and Second Lieutenants would routinely take jobs normally reserved for Captains, or even Majors. And Captain Hamilton was the only officer in the Army Support Services Office. He was overwhelmed with the workload, and desperately wanted help.

I explained to Captain Hamilton that I had been assigned a Postal MOS (military occupational specialty). But he was undeterred. "Come on," he said. "Let's go see Colonel Kavanaugh".

And off we went to see Colonel Kavanaugh. A few blocks from Captain Hamilton's Army Support Services Office stood a 12-story building (a skyscraper by 1968 Frankfurt standards) called the "Taunus Haus". The headquarters of Support District Hessen were located in the Taunus Haus. Colonel Kavanagh was actually a Lieutenant Colonel, and he served as the Deputy Commander of Support District Hessen. The Commander of the Support District was a full Colonel, but Kavanagh was the man who oversaw the day-to-day operations. The Commander may have been the face of the Support District and he interfaced with the General who was the Corp Commander, but it was Kavanagh who made all the decisions.

LTC Kavanagh was a tall man with a slight paunch and a full head of gray hair. He walked with a slight limp – perhaps a battle injury or a civilian trip-and-fall. In mannerisms he was a bit folksy and a bit crude, in retrospect reminding me of a Lyndon Johnson – ready to lift his shirt to show you the scar from his operation. He had an easy manner, and seemed to be a kind-hearted man. He fully realized that he had peaked in his Army career and this assignment as Deputy Commander of the Support District, and his rank as Lieutenant Colonel, would be as far as he could or would go in the military.

Captain Hamilton had an easy relationship with LTC Kavanagh and the Captain arrived, with me in tow, without an appointment. After the introductions, Captain Hamilton made a full court pitch that the work of the Army Support Services was burgeoning and he needed another officer to help him meet the demands. They spoke for a good 15 minutes, and at the conclusion of the conference, LTC Kavanagh told Captain Hamilton that he would give his suggestion his consideration. I noticed that it was not a firm commitment.

And so, I went to work for Captain Hamilton as his deputy. But in the meantime, my wife had secured passage on a commercial flight and she came over to Frankfurt to join me. One advantage in working for Army Support Services is that I had access to a lot of contacts to provide housing. I secured temporary housing for us in a military housing complex that was composed of converted German apartments. We were given a suite of rooms at the very top attic floor. It turned out to be a connection of about 10 rooms – far more than we could ever need. We lived in a couple of the rooms, and closed the interconnecting doors to the others. That sojourn was short-lived, however. Lea and I decided we did not want to live in military housing nor on any military base. We wanted to live "on the economy" – this is Army slang for living in German housing in the German economy. Very few military personnel did that (it was much more secure on base), but we decided that with my knowledge of German and our duty in downtown Frankfurt, that made sense.

Through Army Support Services I found a young sergeant who had been living in a German apartment building about three blocks from the center of Frankfurt, on a mixed-use street called Bornwiesenweg. He was finishing up his military assignment and was being rotated back to the States. I made arrangements to take over his apartment and his lease, brought in some more furniture from the Army Support Services warehouse, and Lea and I took up residence in downtown Frankfurt.

It turned out to be a wonderful arrangement. The apartment building was fairly new, quite clean, with five stories and a modest elevator. We lived on the third floor with a nice view of the streetscape. On the ground floor there were two retail establishments

– a tailor shop and a small laundromat – very convenient. The rest of the neighborhood consisted of apartment buildings with commercial and retail on the ground floor. Across the street from us was a small butcher shop, a tobacconist/bookstore, a small Gasthaus (restaurant/beer hall), a flower shop, and other establishments where one could shop for one's daily needs. At the corner was a moveable hot dog vendor who served assorted German and Polish sausages, French fries (with mayonnaise as the Germans preferred), and curry ketchup. A short three-block walk from our quarters brought us right to the very center of the downtown shopping district of Frankfurt – a place that Lea and I often frequented.

Our apartment was small – basically just a living room and a bedroom, with a tiny kitchen and a tiny bathroom. The refrigerator, stove and oven, kitchen sink, matched the kitchen in size – all Lilliputian. The living room, however, had a large window with a view of the quaint streetscape. The small bedroom faced the back and was very quiet. It was a bright and sunny little apartment – and it suited us nicely.

I joined the Officers Club which was located in a massive old German building which was located immediately behind an even more massive building called the IG Farben building – both structures dated from years before the war and were miraculously undamaged. Lea found herself a job in the Officers Club as a cashier. She loved it. During the day she would work as the cashier in the dining hall and then as a cashier in the slot machine room. A social animal by nature, Lea enjoyed meeting and chatting with the other officers who frequented the club. What she particularly enjoyed, however, is that she was paid in German Marks (the currency used before the Euro was adopted) which had an exchange rate of one Dollar for four Marks. This was a remarkably favorable rate if you were an American. For example, you could purchase an excellent dinner in a Gasthaus for as little as six Marks ($1.50). And Lea could buy shoes on the economy for as little as 24 Marks ($6.00). The Officers Club was a hangout for us. I was elected as a member of the Board of Directors of the Club – the youngest officer ever so elected.

I recall one holiday season, at New Year's, the Officer's Club threw a big blow out New Year's Eve Party. Lea and I attended, of course, and had a very nice time. However, I celebrated too much, and frankly, had too much to drink. It was the second, and last, time in my life that I was drunk. But, young and foolish, we got in my car (at the time, an older model Mercedes) and drove from the Officer's Club to our home on Bornwiesenweg. It was winter, very cold, and streets were covered with ice and snow. We made it home, safe. But as I reflected back on this experience the next day, I realized that I had a recollection of getting in the car at the Club and then arriving home at the apartment – and absolutely no recollection of the time in between. It is a small miracle that Lea and I made it home that night. I was certainly young and stupid – but I learned my lesson. I have never drunk to excess since that time.

Since Lea was working, she rightfully wanted her own car to get to and from work. I asked her what kind of car she wanted and she said a Volkswagen. I think she was thinking of one of those traditional "beetles". But I got her a hatchback because I thought it was safer, roomier and more practical. I got it in British racing green. Lea tooled around in her VW hatchback and I drove the old Benz.

My Adjutant Generals Corps graduating class, Fort Benjamin Harrison, 1968. There I am, front row, third from the left.

Sixteen

Suddenly I'm a Special Services Officer

Over the next two months I worked with Captain Hamilton at Army Support Services and actually got into the job. It was good work, there was plenty of it, and I felt that I was doing something to help soldiers and their families. I threw myself into the work. But, barely into the job, I got a call from LTC Kavanaugh's office – the Colonel wanted to see me right away. So, I went over to the Taunus Haus to see the Colonel. When I got to his office, he was not alone. There was a very tall officer by the name of Captain Irwin in the office with Kavanaugh. In addition to his height, he was noteworthy because his hair was about as long as one could wear it in the Army of 1968. To cut right to the chase, I was informed that the Captain was finishing his tour of duty and was transferring back to the States. LTC Kavanaugh needed to replace the Captain, and he decided that I would be the one. The colonel informed me that I would be the new Special Services Officer for all military and dependents in the German State of Hessen.

And so, in the span of weeks I had gone from Postal Officer, to Army Community Services Officer, to Special Services Officer. At the time, I had only a generalized notion of what a Special Services Officer did. I knew, from basic training, that Special Services was within the job description for the Adjutant Generals Corp, but it was the smallest function of the AGC. The AGC was the smallest branch of the Army, comprising about 1% of the officers in the Army, and Special Services was smallest division with the AGC, comprising about 1% of that branch. My new Military Occupational Specialty (MOS) was now 5000, and I realized that I had arrived in very rarified atmosphere. Captain Hamilton was certainly not thrilled to lose his deputy, but there was nothing he could do – and he graciously wished me well.

As the Special Services Officer, my domain in Hessen was huge, particularly for a 22-year-old Second Lieutenant. I was responsible for almost 200 facilities and close to 250 employees. The employees were almost all American or German civilians; I only had about 30 military assigned to me. In sum, I was responsible for all the libraries, service clubs, movie theaters, entertainment centers, arts-and-craft shops, auto shops, bowling alleys, gymnasiums and sports facilities, and teen clubs. In addition, I had a "tours office" under my jurisdiction, and I was further responsible for any traveling USO shows that might happen to wander into Hessen. The civilians who worked for me were all professionals in their fields, and each unit was headed by a GS-10, GS-11, GS-12, or GS-13 – in other words, high-level professional recreation supervisors. My main assistant was a Sergeant First Class who spent most of his time inspecting the local racket ball court. My main contacts were with the GS-10's, GS-11's, GS-12's and GS-13's who ran the show.

I moved from the quaint Army Community Services Office to the Taunus Haus, and occupied an office one floor down from LTC Kavanaugh. Special Services took up the entire floor. The proximity allowed me to develop a close working relationship with the colonel. He would often call me to accompany him on his walk-abouts. My daily routine involved meetings with my senior staff and signing a great number of requisitions and reports. But, frankly, most of my time was spent on the road, inspecting facilities and making sure the personnel in the field were doing their jobs. It was heady work for a young Second Lieutenant. The job should rightfully have been filled by a Major or a Captain. However, due to the buildup in Viet Nam, the work was necessarily given to a Second Lieutenant – me.

My time was pretty much my own. Other than the occasions when duty called (e.g. walks with LTC Kavanaugh) I was left to my own devices. I would meet regularly with my senior staff. Rarely, however, did the GS's encounter a problem that they couldn't handle. These were people who had been doing what they were doing for 10, 15, 20 years. The were pros. I signed my name to a LOT of papers. In fact, it was during this time of my life, my early 20's, that I developed the unique somewhat bold signature that I would use for the rest of my life. When not in the office, I would take the time to visit and "inspect" the facilities and personnel assigned to Special Services throughout the state of Hessen. As noted, there were well over 200 such facilities scattered in small bases and Kasernes throughout that German state.

One other duty not otherwise assigned was to handle USO tours that happened to stop in Frankfurt. There weren't many of them as the great bulk of those tours entertained troops in safer areas of Vietnam. But I did handle a couple of them. One such tour featured Bob Hope, and I had the pleasure of watching the great entertainer from the wings. I must say, however, my main impression of his act was not a favorable one. He was the master of the one liner, and I recall from the wings seeing aides holding up a series of large cards, each containing the one-liner he would speak next. I also recall him playing to the cameras, and not the audience – so he would often stop and redo the line (again and again) till he felt he had gotten it just right. While this all troubled me, it didn't seem to bother the audience who simply enjoyed seeing the great comedian up close and personal.

I spent a fair amount of time in the unique "Tours Office" that was under my jurisdiction in the IG Farben building. This particular office was planted right in the middle of the great lobby of that building and it was run by a somewhat eccentric Hungarian by the name of Jules Gyori. Mr. Gyori somehow was always able to snag some opera tickets for Lea and me, and he also introduced us to palacinka – a wonderful Slavic dessert. Once, Mr. Gyori even managed to organize a trip for Lea and me to visit the Adriatic Coast of Italy – to the lovely town of Rimini. We stayed at the Grand Hotel Rimini, had a wonderful time, and managed to totally sunburn our bodies.

The tours office also organized amazing trips for members of the service and their families. Working with Mr. Gyori, I organized a number of one-day excursions throughout our part of Europe. Distances on the continent are much shorter than in the States, and efficient trains ran everywhere. So, we would rent entire trains just for Special Services and fill them up with soldiers, and their families. We took excursions to Luxemburg, Strassburg, Rothenberg, Dinkelsbuhl, Nurnberg and other wonderful locations. We would enjoy the train ride, see the sights, eat the food, drink the beer and return back to Frankfurt at the end of the day – tired and very happy. In this way, I was able to expose young soldiers and their families to a Europe they would not normally see. And there was no charge for the train trip. Lea, in particular, loved the short day trips (we went on every one) and I'm pretty sure none of the other European Special Services Officers thought of organizing trips like this during their tours of duty.

After a year in Germany, I was promoted to First Lieutenant. Nothing particularly special about that – it was a routine promotion. Toward the end of my two-year tour of duty, LTC Kavanaugh strongly encouraged me to sign up for one more year and he promised me a promotion to Captain. I thought about it – a military career held some appeal for me. But ultimately I declined. Frankly, I was not keen on spending another year where I would certainly be sent to Viet Nam and where it was quite possible that I would wind up as a Postal Officer once again. Not that I would be in any particular personal danger. Members of the Adjutant Generals Corps were not in combat and certainly weren't on the front lines. Plus, I had no desire to separate from my wife for a year. So, I decided that my Army career would begin and end in Germany. As a parting touch, the Army presented me with an Army Commendation Medal (the ARCOM) which was just about the highest medal I could receive for this sort of non-combat duty.

But now what? I knew that I wanted to go back to school and obtain an advanced degree. But what degree? The three options I considered were a PhD in mass communication based on my love of journalism, or an M.D. like both of Lea's parents, or a law degree. After talking it over with Lea as well as Lea's parents, I made a decision. I was quite interested in the degree in mass communication, but decided that – in the 1960's journalism was just about the lowest-paying profession around and Lea and

I were ready to have a child. Lea's mother, Genevieve, asked me if I was skilled in math and science, and I certainly was not. My skills were more in English and social sciences. She advised that medical school would be very difficult for me without the aptitude in math and science. So, law school was the inevitable choice.

There was one hurdle, however. To attend law school, I had to take and pass the Law School Aptitude Test (LSAT). This test was known to be the second hardest test that anyone had to endure in order to obtain a law degree (second only to the Bar Exam which had to be passed after law school for the privilege of practicing law). And passing the LSAT was required to be accepted to any decent law school. So, I made arrangements to take that test. Not necessarily easy as I was in Germany. But I discovered that the LSAT was offered in Germany – however, only in Heidelberg, not in Frankfurt. I registered for the test and then took the three-hour drive to Heidelberg on a Saturday. The test was offered at an Army base in Heidelberg early in the morning hours. I have always been an early riser so this was no problem for me. And, as usual, I had given myself a generous amount of time to drive to Heidelberg, plus some extra time for unforeseen traffic. I arrived in Heidelberg on time, but then found that I was completely lost in that rather large city. This was a time before GPS, and I was hopelessly adrift on the roads of Heidelberg. Like most German towns, they were not laid out in a simple grid system. Rather, streets and alleys connected at odd angles depending on where the medieval wagon wheels had run. But the gods must have been with me that day because I had an epiphany. I flagged down a taxi driver, gave him the address I needed, and told him that I would follow him in my car to the location. Fortunately, he agreed, and we made the loop to the Army base where the test was administered. I paid the taxi and actually made it to the test site with a few minutes to spare (always a good idea to use the restroom before one starts a big test). Close call for me, but had I not made it, my law school career – and perhaps my life's path – would have been delayed at least a year.

Because my two-year Army commitment would end in the winter of 1970 and law school wouldn't start till the fall of 1971,

I had a gap of time to fill. Lucky me. I was able to negotiate a six-month temporary civil service assignment with the Army as a GS-7 to work as an "advisor" to my successor as Special Services Officer. While it was a little bit strange to one day be in charge, and the next day to be an advisor to the person in charge, it worked out and it paid the bills. My replacement was another Second Lieutenant who had brought his wife over, and the four of us got along quite well for those six months.

In 1968-69 I became a Special Services Officer, serving in Europe. Here I am as a young Second Lieutenant, taking "command" of Special Services from my predecessor, Captain Irwin.

*In 1969 I was ensconced in the Taunus Haus in
Frankfurt, running a large Special Services operation for
the Army. It was a great job!*

Seventeen

My Life in Law School

Applying to law school from Germany was not particularly easy. This was, after all, 1970 – well before computers and web sites. The local Special Services library in Frankfurt had a few law school catalogues, and that's what I relied on. I knew that I wanted to go back to California. So with that starting point, I applied to four law schools: two in Southern California and two in Northern California. My knowledge of law schools in California could fill a thimble. But I read the catalogues and hoped that they provided accurate information. Ultimately, I was accepted to two of the law schools – the two in the northern part of the state. One of them was the University of California, Hastings College of the Law in San Francisco – an old and prestigious institution in the middle of the city. The other was a very new law school, also part of the University of California, in the small town of Davis, in Yolo County. It was quite a stark choice.

On the one hand, Hastings had history and panache and all the large and powerful law firms had offices in San Francisco. On the other hand, Davis had an appeal being on the ground floor of a brand new school of law. Which to choose? When Lea and I got back to the States in 1971, we visited both. Hastings turned out to be a series of gray buildings surrounded by more gray buildings. It was very urban. Davis was a small, bucolic town. When the University of California opened its general campus there in the early 1900's, it was known as "The University Farm." The law school had held its first graduation in 1969 less than a year earlier than my application. The law school building, itself, was relatively small (compared to Hastings) but it was set next to a wandering creek and the Arboretum – a vast ribbon of greenery and trees running for miles through the campus. The entering class

at Hastings would have close to 400 students; at Davis the entering class would be around 150.

Ultimately, another discussion with Lea's folks helped me
make my decision. By the time I had to decide, Lea was pregnant
and would be giving birth in the Fall. Genevieve – ever with wise
counsel – suggested that it would be cheaper to find housing in
Davis (rather than San Francisco) and it would be a better place to
raise a child. So, we opted for the law school at UC Davis, eventually to be named Martin Luther King Jr. School of Law – and
as we came to know it "King Hall". In retrospect, this decision
of location was critical to the path of my life (although I didn't
realize it at the time). Had I chosen Hastings, I'm sure that my
life's path would have taken me to one of the larger law firms
and I would have wound up ensconced in corporate law, with a
suburban home, and a daily commute to and from San Francisco.
As it turned out, by choosing Davis – a 20-minute drive to the
State Capitol in Sacramento – my life's path would inevitably take
me into government and politics. But that's a story for another
chapter.

So, Lea and I accepted admission to King Hall in Davis, and
we moved to that town in the summer of 1971. I emphasize the
word "summer." Lea and I arrived in town in the middle of the
summer, in preparation for start of the law school year in September. We packed up our car, and drove into Davis – at the time
with a population under 35,000 – and as is my wont we drove
through downtown looking for an apartment to rent. I actually
found an apartment within minutes of arriving in the downtown.
The central core of Davis is laid out in a traditional grid system –
something that is rare in Western towns. Davis had a grid running
north-south with A Street, B Street, C Street and so on. And the
grid continued east-west with First Street, Second Street, Third
Street, etc. I found an apartment on First Street, between D and E
Streets. It was a small unit that contained perhaps 12 apartments.
Ours was on the second floor, overlooking First Street. The apartment was spare and simple. Basically, just a living room, kitchen,
bathroom and one bedroom. It was furnished, which was helpful

for a young couple just starting out.

My first introduction to Davis was bringing Lea up to the second floor of a little apartment in 100 degree heat. We were hot and tired and very pregnant. Poor Lea sat on the bed and just cried. Welcome to Davis.

But, it got better. Davis was a town where you can exist quite well without a car. Money was not a particular problem for us. I had the financial support of the GI Bill which provided us a few hundred dollars a month while I attended law school. I also worked at various odd jobs during my three-year stint in law school. These jobs included work as a stringer for the local newspaper (the Davis Enterprise), paid by the column inch. I even developed a "question man" column for the paper, and did the photography myself. Lea's parents provided a measure of financial support as well. My parents were still alive, but not in a position to provide much help in the way of funds. All in all, we did surprisingly well.

One of the great events of my life occurred during that first year of law school. In November of 1971, our son, Jason was born. A good-looking boy, Jason was a major addition to our young family. Of course, having a baby while in law school was no picnic for either Lea or me – but we were a little more mature than the average new parents, and we did fine. He was an energetic and happy baby and we were quite proud of him. It took him a long time to sleep through the night, and for many months we would take turns getting up at 2 a.m. to feed him. Lea breast fed so my job was easy – I would just get up, get Jason, plop him next to Lea and then pass out again. Sometimes I forgot to put him back in his bed, and found him the next morning ensconced by Lea, happy as a clam.

Soon after he was born we moved into a house, with substantial financial help from Lea's parents, Herman and Genevieve. We built a tract home in a new East Davis neighborhood. I remember the cost of that house was $21,500 – but we actually paid $23,500 because we pushed out two walls to make the rooms a bit bigger. That seemed like a great deal of money then, but today you can easily spend more than that just for a car. Jason spent his early years in that house located at 2828 Loyola Drive. About a year after Jason was born, we were pregnant again, but Lea miscarried. And then soon thereafter, we were pregnant yet again. Another fine boy was born who we brought home and named Justin. I was very happy to have a second child. But the happiness turned to despair within days. Justin was only with us for a short time – a matter of days really. We brought Justin home and he lived with us briefly, but he had a bad heart. And he died. Losing two children – one from a miscarriage and one from a bad heart – hit me hard. But I am sure it hit Lea even harder. Both little boys are buried in the Davis Cemetery. Parents should never have to bury their children – it just doesn't seem right.

I readily took to law school. I was no dummy, having graduated college with a 3.4 GPA (in the days before grade inflation). I had been on the Dean's List and President's List at Cal Poly on a regular basis, and I had the benefit of two years working for the Army. So, I was a couple of years older (and more mature) than the typical law school student. But law school can be and was a shock to the system of many students. You see, everyone in law school had been a top student while in college. They were accustomed to getting the best grades and to being the smartest kids in class. Well, law school brought all those great brains together in one class. And law school graded on a curve. So, while some would be at the top, others would be in the middle, or even the bottom of the curve. That was devastating to some. I, however, thrived in the competitive milieu of law school.

I think the secret of success to law school is being organized. Everyone in law school is smart – so we all start on an even plane in the way of brains. But not everyone is organized. I was uber-organized. I used my time productively and well. I still recall seeing students working in the law library from morning till night – sitting in library carrels poring over the books and releasing a heavy sigh from time to time. I never did that. I used the time between classes to study, and I rarely studied at night. Instead, I would be home with Lea making dinner, taking walks through the downtown – living a normal life. Also, I found virtually every law student belonged to a "study group.' These groups would meet often – some even daily – to study together, help each other out, and answer questions that group members had about the reading, the case or the assignment. I tried a study group once or twice, and never did it again. I did not find it was a productive use of my time. Seems like I would spend my time answering questions of the other students. So, I stopped attending the study group, and became a study group of one.

Make no mistake about it. Law school is a slog. If you are a fulltime student, like I was, it takes three years to make it through the curriculum. Making it through requires perseverance, patience and fortitude. The first year of law school is a series of required courses – learning the basics of the law – property, contracts, torts, criminal law, legal research and writing. We had no computers in 1971. We just had books. Lots and lots of books. The second and third years provided a bit more flexibility – there were courses required to be taken. But there were also electives where students – to the extent that they had an inclination and an interest – could sign up – family law, juvenile law. jurisprudence. Law school classes – particularly in the first year – are taught in the Socratic Method. This is a method which drives law students crazy. In the Socratic method, the instructor never really answers questions. Instead, the instructor teaches by asking questions to the students. "Mr. Rosenberg, you read the Sanchez case in last evening's assignment. What do you believe to be the main holding in that case?" And Rosenberg would spout off for a while. And then the instructor would turn to another student and ask, "Do you agree with Mr. Rosenberg?" In this painstaking and slow methodology we would learn, and more importantly, we would learn to think for ourselves, and to express ourselves logically as advocates.

Because King Hall was a new law school, our class sizes were small – about 150 students – compared to other law schools where each class might number 300, 400 or more students. And we were diverse. King Hall prided itself on a diverse student body and a diverse faculty. We had a very high percentage of women and ethnic minority students in my class – and in the classes that followed mine. It was an honor to participate in a legal education with students that reflected the community at large.

In my third year, the school (at least in those days) allowed students to create their own student-run seminars. Although this was rarely attempted, and even rarer still, accomplished – I did it. I created a student-run seminar entitled "Law and Journalism." It was a pleasure combining my twin interests in law and the press into one program. We had about a dozen students sign up for it. There was no faculty – only students. Each student took a turn in presenting and leading one class. This is where I first met Bob Dunning, who would become a life-long "enemy" and "friend" – but more about that later. Bob was one year ahead of me in law school. I was the Class of 1974 (the year of my graduation) and Bob was the Class of 1973. I had not met Bob before the seminar, but I had heard of him. Bob was actually a bit of a legend at King Hall. He was known as never attending any classes. Bob would simply show up for the tests, and apparently did well enough, as he passed the tests and moved on to the next year. The seminar on Law and Journalism seemed to be an exception. Bob attended many of the seminar sessions, and I found him to be a complex and interesting fellow.

Throughout my three years of law school, I kept really good notes in every class. I focused those notes on what I perceived I would be asked on the State Bar Exam. I knew from the get-go that whatever we did in law school was fine, but at the conclusion of law school, one had to pass a three-day examination to be able to actually practice law. (I had a friend in law school who graduated in my class of 1974, but never could pass that exam, even after a half-dozen tries. He is a law graduate who cannot practice law. I believe he wound up working in real estate.) So, with the goal in mind of the Bar Exam, my note-taking and studying focused on what I believed I would face on the Bar Exam. I saved all my notes, and then at the conclusion of three years of law school, I spent the bulk of my time preparing for that exam by reading and re-reading my notes. Oh, I took a Bar Exam Prep course. Everyone does that to be on the safe side. But I found my personal notes to be of much more help on that exam.

While in law school from 1971 to 1974, the majority of my time was spent in my studies or with Lea and Jason. I also devoted some time working for some solo practitioner lawyers as a legal researcher and writer. They paid by the hour and I could earn some pretty decent money. Extracurricular activities, necessarily, were few. I remember joining the ACLU and actually becoming president of the Yolo County chapter of the ACLU. I also joined the National Organization for Women (NOW) to support women's rights, and held that membership for decades. In law school I participated in Moot Court where students make appellate arguments on various subjects to mock appellate judges. I even won one of those competitions with some arguments I presented on copyright law. I found that I enjoyed Trial Practice more than Moot Court. In Moot Court you argue appellate cases (all legal arguments) to a Court of Appeal or Supreme Court. In Trial Practice, you participated as trial counsel before a Superior Court Judge, so it is mostly facts and evidence, not dry legal arguments. I also used my Special Service experience to name and organize the "Cardozorama" – a talent show where law students could display their skills in singing, dancing, musical instruments and the like. I was the first director of this show. Much to my surprise, when I returned to the law school some 20 years after my graduation, I saw posters in the hallways advertising the "Cardozorama" – I was amazed to see that my crazy idea with the crazy name had resonated and was continuing.

Overall, I did pretty well in law school, graduating #2 in my Class of 1974. Because of my standing in my class, I was chosen to be a law clerk for a Federal District Judge. I was hired to work as a law clerk for Thomas J. MacBride, the Chief Judge of the United States District Court for the Eastern District of California, based in Sacramento. The Eastern District was the largest, geographically, in the state, covering about two-thirds of California. It was to be a two-year commitment from 1974 to 1976. Those law clerk positions are coveted and are considered the top of the food chain for new graduates. They are typically filled very early in the job hunt process. That selection happened toward the end of my second year of law school. So, while all my classmates spent much of their third year on the hunt for a post-graduation job, I was all set up to start the clerkship after graduation.

My father Harry and mother Fay with Jason

Eighteen

A Toe in the Political Waters

And another event occurred in my third year of law school that would have a profound effect on my life. I had tracked local, state and national politics a bit, but nothing beyond that point. In 1973-74, however, I became intrigued with a young rising star in state politics – Jerry Brown. At the time, I was 27 years old, and Jerry was 35. He was California Secretary of State – a relatively benign position – but one which he energized by vigorously enforcing the new Political Reform Act. I liked his energy, his focus on honesty and frugality, and his charisma. So, I jumped in with both feet – contacted the campaign and said I wanted to volunteer to help. Well, I got more than I bargained for. Two campaign aides by the names of Jim Mulligan and Arden McConnell contacted me, and next thing I knew I was designated as the campaign chairman for the County of Yolo campaign for Jerry Brown for Governor.

I was young and inexperienced in politics, but I had enthusiasm and drive, and I applied myself to the campaign. It was a challenging task. There were five legitimate candidates for the Democratic Primary election for Governor in that election of 1974 – far more than is usually seen. The candidates included Secretary of State Jerry Brown, San Francisco Mayor Joe Alioto, Assembly Speaker Bob Moretti, liberal Congressman Jerry Waldie, and multi-millionaire William Matson Roth. We ran a vigorous Jerry Brown campaign in Yolo County. The Democratic establishment of the county rallied behind Roth (of all people) and Jerry was viewed as an outsider and somewhat of a radical. In the county, Roth squeaked out a narrow victory over Jerry (who came in a close second in Yolo). But statewide, Jerry crushed his opponents – mostly from the support of the south state. He went on to win the governorship, beating State Controller Houston Flournoy. Jerry got a shade over 50% of the general election vote to Flourney's 47%. In the general election, Brown received 54% of the vote in Yolo County – 8th highest out of 58 counties. And so, Jerry Brown, at the ripe young age of 36, was elected Governor of the State of California. I went to a number of rallies and functions where I saw Jerry from a distance, and during the campaign, had occasion to meet him only one time. He came to the UC Davis campus for a rally, and Jim Mulligan introduced Jerry to me. Jerry, ever the iconoclast, greeted me, but never said "hello" – his only words to me that day were, "You're so pale." And I guess I was. But there will be more about Jerry later in this work as he became a major part of my early life.

On balance, I had a pleasurable experience in law school and I inhaled the knowledge offered to me at King Hall. The class that I enjoyed the most was Jurisprudence – the philosophy of law. The class where I received my lowest grade in law school (my one and only B minus) was Criminal Procedure. Ironically, that is the arena where I spent much of my life as a Judge – in the criminal courts. Life moves in mysterious ways.

However, just graduating law school does not allow one to practice law. There is yet another hurdle – and it's a big one. You have to take and pass that state's Bar Exam. There are few tests that are tougher than the Bar Exam. It's a three-day ordeal that you have to prepare for mentally, physically and emotionally. The first two days consist of a series of essay questions, each focused on a different area of the law – property, torts, contracts, criminal law, conflict of laws, and the like. The essays test your ability to identify the issues presented by the question, and then to discuss the ramifications of the issues. The correct "answer" to the question, I suspect, is less important that the proper and comprehensive identification and discussion of the issues. The third day of the Bar Exam is the so-called "multi-state" exam part – this is a test that many states have adopted as part of their Bar Exam. The questions are presented not as essay questions, but rather as multiple choice questions. Four answers are given, and the test taker has to choose which one is correct. To me, the multi-state exam was much harder than the essay exam. For each multiple choice question, I could quickly eliminate two of the proposed answers, and then I was left with two remaining options, often going in opposite directions – and it was difficult for me to pick one. And that's because many things in the law are not black and white (like they are in mathematics) – they often present shades and nuances. And while I could readily discern the issues presented by the question, it was not as easy to pick the correct answer without the opportunity to discuss those shades and nuances.

The California Bar Exam is given twice a year in several cities throughout the state, each in a very large room or auditorium. I took the exam given in the summer of 1974 at the Court of Appeals building in Downtown Sacramento. It seemed to me that there were several hundred people in the room. This was the mid-70's so there were no laptops. You could take the exam using a pen or you could type the exam on an electric typewriter. The vast majority of the test takers opted for a pen, and so did I. (I pity the bar examiners who had to read all those hand-written answers, often written, or scribbled, in haste.) In the very back of the room was a row of test takers using electric typewriters. The exam is timed. The proctors told us to begin and we dived right in.

Here are some of my impressions. First, when the proctors told us to start I noticed, with my peripheral vision, several people who began to write in their exam books almost immediately. How they were able to do that without even reading the question is beyond me. I guess they had so much accumulated information in their brains that they just had to let the regurgitation begin. Second, after about ten minutes, I noticed a handful of test takers slowly close their test books, pick up their papers, and quietly walk out of the room. Never saw them again. I imagine these were the folks who looked at a question or two and decided that they were not going to do well on that exam at this time. Third, after about an hour into the exam, the sound of typing in the back row just stopped. Horror of horrors – there was a power outage at the Court of Appeals building. I kept writing with my trusty pen. But the entire back row looked like they had been hit with seizures. People were jumping up and down, waving frantically for the proctors, and doing their best impressions of the St. Vitus' Dance. Mercifully, the power came back on after about 15-20 minutes, but it appeared to me that several of the test typists were thrown off their game. Such are the stories of the Bar Exam.

The Bar Examiners don't tell you how you did on the exam – just whether you passed or not. I passed. But I will never know if I passed with a score of 70% or 99%. But then, who really cares, as long as you pass. Taking the exam more than once is not uncommon. And many smart men and women, who become top-notch lawyers, have failed the first time but passed the second time. Governor Jerry Brown (who is one of the smartest men I have ever known) passed the exam on the second go-round.

Because most of the exam is in the essay format – with a lot of writing – the grading takes a fair amount of time and the results are not posted for several months. Typically, for the summer exam, result will be posted around Thanksgiving – which for the test-takers becomes a time of either joy or despair. So, folks begin their first post-law-school jobs in September, not knowing if they are real lawyers until sometime in November. And, for those who get their test results showing that they did not pass, it can be the ultimate downer in their lives. Sometimes, those first employers will let you stay on and will give you a second crack at the exam (which is also offered in the Spring). But sometimes they just let you go. And if you don't pass that second time around, they always ask you to move on. If one attends an accredited law school, the pass rate on the Bar Exam is traditionally high. If one attends an unaccredited law school (which many law students do) the pass rate is traditionally low. And for some of these students who worked all through law school, they attend night school which is normally a process that takes four years (rather than the traditional three years). I can only imagine the disappointment, the shattering of dreams, for the students who worked all day and went to law school all night, only to take and fail the Bar Exam. I was blessed to be able to jump all these hurdles, and get sworn in as an Attorney and Counselor at Law in California in November of 1974.

The Bar Examiners of the State of California was formed in 1929 and started issuing Bar numbers at that time. The Bar issues those Bar numbers in sequence. In other words, the very first lawyer admitted to the Bar in California was the Supreme Court Chief Justice at the time – William H. Waste. He received Bar Number 1. In one of my law firms I worked with a lawyer who had a Bar number in the 17,000's. My Bar number is in the 61,000's. Young lawyers today receive Bar numbers in the 300,000's.

King Hall does an interesting thing with its alumni. In five-year increments, the alumni are invited back to the law school to mingle with classmates, be feted, and (of course) be pitched to make alumni contributions. So, as a member of the Class of 1974, I was invited to attend this law school alumni gatherings in 1979, 1984, 1989, 1994, 1999, 2004, 2009, 2014, and 2019. I believe I have been able to attend all of them. At these reunions, all classes in five year increments attend. So, for example, in the gathering of 2019, not only did my class of 1974 attend, but also the class of 1969 (the very first graduating class of King Hall), but also the Classes of 1979, 1984, 1989, etc. That gathering in 2019 was re-markably weird for me because the only ones attending from the Class of 1974 were two of my classmates and me (plus Lea). We had the smallest turnout of any of the feted classes. The next one will be particularly interesting because 2024 will mark my 50th law school Class reunion. I certainly hope to be there. Perhaps I will be the last man standing from my class and toast myself with a bottle of wine.

So 1974 was a memorable year for me. I graduated law school in 1974 with a Juris Doctor degree, took and passed the Bar Exam, and was ready to take on the world of law.

The obligatory campaign photo. Lea and Dave.

Nineteen

An Interlude with the Federal Court

On Capitol Mall in Downtown Sacramento, California, with a direct view of the State Capitol Building just four blocks away, sits a squat three-story, mustard-colored building housing the Federal Courthouse. Or it did in 1974. The building is still there housing federal offices – but has been replaced as the federal courthouse by a sleek, marble modern skyscraper. Apparently, money is no object when Federal buildings are involved and when the mint prints the money for them.

In 1974, however, the mustard building was the seat of federal judicial power. This was the headquarters of the United States District Court for the Eastern District of California, a huge district covering, geographically, well over half the State of California. In the mid-70's three Federal District Judges held court in this building, including the Chief Judge Thomas J. MacBride, appointed by President John F. Kennedy. A fourth District Judge sat in Fresno. In addition to the District Judges, the building housed offices for Justice Anthony Kennedy, at the time a Justice of the 9th Circuit Court of Appeals – this was prior to his appointment to the Supreme Court of the United States where he became an influential moderate, often serving as the crucial fifth vote deciding cases at SCOTUS.

In addition to the courts, the building housed a number of federal offices, including the Office of the U.S. Attorney, the Federal Defender's Office, an extensive Clerk's Office, a Magistrate, court reporters, and court security. It was an important and self-contained world, and the seat of Federal judicial authority in Sacramento and much of the surrounding land.

I walked into this world as my very first job out of law school. During my second year in law school, I had accepted a two-year commitment as a Law Clerk to Tom MacBride. The way it worked is that every Federal District Judge was allotted two Law Clerks, who typically, served overlapping two-year stints. Serving as a Law Clerk out of law school was a prestigious position, as the Judges picked only the best of the best. On Day One of my new tenure, I met with Millie, the tall lanky, no-nonsense woman who served as the Judge's Secretary, who immediately ushered me in to see the Judge, himself. I recall my very first impression of Judge MacBride was of his chambers. The Judge was dwarfed by this chambers. Frankly, I had never in my life seen an office of the size of Judge MacBride's chambers. They were huge, and festooned with plaques, awards, pictures, and wall-hangings of his many career accomplishments and honors. Although attired in shirtsleeves and a tie, the man, himself, had a patrician bearing – tall, slender, pants and shirt well-pressed, gray-haired and both jovial and reserved. He was very much into duck hunting and his favorite hunting dog was invariably in the room with him. Judge MacBride greeted me with warmth, but was careful to maintain a certain "distance" from his Law Clerks. I learned that lesson early when I suggested one day that we might have lunch together. "Admirals don't eat with Ensigns," he had responded, matter-of-factly. And that was that. It was not a put-down by Tom MacBride – it was just the way of his world. Instead, he would often lunch with Justice Kennedy – an equally affable man of the same generation as Judge MacBride. They often "hung out" together. I suppose if you are a Federal Judge in Sacramento, there are precious few folks with whom you can just hang out. And I enjoyed the few occasions on which I met and chatted with Justice Kennedy. He was an approachable and humble man, rightfully proud of his Sacramento roots.

After meeting Chief Judge MacBride, I was introduced to the other Law Clerk, Steve Felderstein, with whom I would maintain a life-long friendship. Steve took me to my office and generally filled me in about the job of Law Clerk. MacBride's Law Clerks had overlapping terms so at any given year, one would be the "senior" clerk and the other would be the "junior" clerk. In 1974, when I started, I was the junior clerk – Steve had started in 1973 and was the senior clerk. After a year, in 1975, Steve would move on to another job and I would become the senior clerk till 1976. It turned out that Steve and I were both of the Jewish faith – the first Jews hired by Judge MacBride. Why he suddenly decided to hire a Jewish clerk – and then two in a row – was unknown to me. Perhaps it was just the luck of the draw – in his mind we were the best of the lot at the time.

I got to know and like Steve Felderstein. We worked well together, had lunch together (Ensigns were permitted to eat with Ensigns) and just naturally hit it off. After our one year together as Law Clerks, our relationship continued in the law – but more on that in another chapter.

My Law Clerk's office was impressive. (At least, I was impressed.) While the Judge's chambers were overwhelming, the Law Clerk's offices were as spacious as any office I was to occupy over the next thirty years. Steve and I had identical private offices, just a few feet down the hall from Judge MacBride's chambers. The windows of our offices looked down on Capitol Mall.

The work of a federal Law Clerk is interesting and varied. The Law Clerk is far more than a researcher of the law. For Judge MacBride, the law clerks had three primary assignments. One job was to give a quick analysis and recommendation on legal or evidentiary issues that might come up during the course of the day in court. The second job was to review decisions of the Magistrate and the Writ Clerk before they were submitted to the Judge. The third task was to write opinions and decisions on legal matters (primarily civil) that the Judge has taken under submission, ultimately for the Judge's signature. This third responsibility was, by far, the most important and also the most challenging.

At the time, and in a typical year, the Judge would take under submission around 50-60 such matters. On most matters, the Judge could and did rule from the Bench. But on those 50-60 matters – due to volume or complexity – the Judge would take the matter under submission. The Law Clerk would keep a list of those submitted matters, and in due course would attend to them, drafting a proposed decision to discuss and finalize with the Judge. I mention this because when I started as a Law Clerk, the slate was not clean. In other words, I didn't find a handful of submitted matters for decision. I found a list of over 60 such matters. These submitted matters ranged from voluminous summary judgment motions, to relatively straight-forward motions to dismiss, to the occasional legal ruling which would decide a case. And some of those matters had languished.

Well, I rolled up my sleeves and attended to this list of submitted cases, many of them which had been "under submission" for a year. By the end of the first year of my two-year Law Clerk commitment, I had whittled that submitted caseload down to zero. And I hasten to add that the submission process did not stand still. During the year I was working to reduce the old caseload, the submitted cases kept coming. So, essentially, at the end of my first year I had handled some 120 matters that needed decisions researched and written. Judge MacBride was impressed and very appreciative – I had taken the waiting time for submitted cases from a year, to a matter of days, when I had finished. I left the next Law Clerk with a submitted caseload of zero.

Because of the special relationship between Judge and Law Clerk, one thing remains kind of confidential. Of course, the Judge signs his/her name on the written decision or opinion. But who actually writes it? Is it the Law Clerk or is it the Judge or is it some combination of both? I have kept that confidence for close to 50 years. But since Judge MacBride passed away decades ago, there is no reason to continue to keep it secret. In fact, I drafted and wrote each and every one of those decisions for the Judge, and he would accept them with few if any minor edits. In fact, in all the decisions that I worked on with Judge MacBride, he and I only disagreed one time. Let me tell you about that one time.

Water has always been a big issue for the Western States, and particularly California. The United States government and the State of California have often been at odds when it comes to the use of water – and agricultural and environmental interests have often clashed on issues relating to water. These matters typically wind up in Court, and usually in the Federal Court system. As the Eastern District of California covers such a huge geographic swath of the State, it is the venue of choice for such disputes. The Mother of All Water Disputes wound up on Judge MacBride's plate during my tenure as his Law Clerk. The case was entitled United States vs. California, and both governments brought their best and their brightest attorneys to the fore to present and argue this case. At stake was a determination of which entity had primacy in the water fight. I had the privilege of sitting through the oral arguments – which were stellar. And then I had the task of writing a draft opinion for the Judge's consideration. It was no mean task. The record was voluminous and the law was complex. Ultimately, I came to the conclusion that the State of California should prevail in this case, and I wrote a lengthy decision (over 80 pages) and presented it to the Judge. He spent some time looking it over and then – a rare event occurred – he disagreed with me. Judge MacBride thought that the United States should prevail based on precedent handed down many years earlier by the U.S. Supreme Court. Of course, he was the Judge, so I re-wrote the opinion in favor of the Federal position, and the decision was signed by the Judge and issued. We are, after all, required to follow precedent.

Naturally, it was understood that whichever side were to lose at the District Court was going to appeal. And that's precisely what occurred. The State of California appealed the decision to the Ninth Circuit Court of Appeals. There were many amicus briefs filed on the case, both pro-State and pro-Federal. The Ninth Circuit, in a unanimous 3-0 decision upheld Judge MacBride. The case was taken up to the U.S. Supreme Court, which decided to hear the matter. Again, amicus briefs flowed like water to that Court. Ultimately, SCOTUS issued a lengthy 6-3 decision reversing the Ninth Circuit (and Judge MacBride), siding with the state. The Supreme Court stepped back from its prior precedent, and in effect, reversed itself – which it had to do to come to its decision. Naturally, no Judge enjoys being reversed, and I certainly never ever said "I told you so." But Judge MacBride took it with style.

He was fond of saying that 13 Judges heard the case and it was 7-6 in favor of Judge MacBride's decision (but the 6, of course, were the 6 that counted).

While United States v. California was the most far-reaching case we handled during my tenure as Law Clerk to Tom Mac-Bride, it was by no means the most sensational case. That "honor" goes to the case of United States vs. Lynnette "Squeaky" Fromme, charged with the attempted assassination of the President of the United States.

In the 1970's Sacramento was by no means a metropolis. Sure, it was the state capital, but in many ways it was still a sleepy little cow town. The tallest building in Sacramento was the State Capitol Building. The main industry in Sacramento was government – state of course, but also federal, county, city, school districts, and a smattering of regional entities. Not much happened in Sacramento in the 1970's. But when the President of the United States visits Sacramento, that's a big event. And that's what happened during my tenure as Law Clerk for Tom MacBride. Gerald Ford, President of the United States, was visiting Sacramento to spend some time with the newly elected Governor of California – Jerry Brown. On September 5, 1975, as President Ford and his entourage were walking across Capitol Park adjacent to the State Capitol, Squeaky Fromme, a member of the Charles Manson Family, got right next to President Ford, pulled out a gun and made as if to shoot the President. Security intervened, the gun did not fire, and President Ford continued to his meeting with the Governor. Fromme was taken into custody and charged with the attempted assassination of the President of the United States. Needless to say, this was a major news event in Sacramento. And the case wound up in Federal Court, assigned to Chief Judge Thomas Mac-Bride, and suddenly our courthouse was surrounded by media. We had the juxtaposition of a President in town, an apparent attempt to shoot him, with the wackiness of the Manson Family thrown in for good measure.

Both Steve Felderstein and I wound up working on the case, assisting the Judge with a myriad of legal issues. The case was prosecuted by Dwayne Keyes, the United States Attorney for the Eastern District of California – a Republican and a fine attorney. For the defense, Judge MacBride appointed Michael Virga, one of the best defense attorneys in the Sacramento Region. One of the first legal issues we confronted was the request by defense to subpoena and interview the President of the United States as a witness in the case. There was remarkably little legal precedents to help up in this area, but ultimately Steve and I offered the Judge a middle ground position. Rather than bring the President to Sacramento for a deposition, we suggested that the attorneys, and the Judge, go to Washington D.C. to depose the President, with the Judge being at the deposition to handle any evidentiary legal issues on the spot. Turned out that was acceptable to all the parties, and also the President. And that's what was done. The case ruling that even the President was subject to the power of the Courts is still on the books and is still authority today.

During the course of the hearings and the trial, I got fairly close to both Dwayne Keyes as well as John Virga, and respected them both. Virga, in particular, felt he had an excellent defense to the serious charge of attempted assassination. He felt that his client was certainly guilty of the crime of assault, but that she was not guilty of the attempted assassination. Virga reasoned that Squeaky's goal was to draw public attention to the teachings and goals of Charlie Manson. She felt that she could draw public attention to Manson as a result of her stunt. Interestingly, the gun never fired because no bullet was chambered. Keyes argued that this was simply an error or oversight by Fromme. Virga felt that she intentionally did not chamber a round because she never intended to assassinate Mr. Ford.

In the beginning, Squeaky – through Virga – argued forcefully that she wanted to subpoena Charles Manson – who was in state prison as a murderer – to be a witness in her case. Clearly, her goal was to see her mentor Manson again, and to give him a forum to present his views about the environment. Ultimately, Judge MacBride, advised by his Law Clerks, decided that Manson could present no relevant evidence in the case and denied Squeaky's request to bring him to Sacramento as a witness. When the Judge issued his ruling, Squeaky immediately shut down and flatly refused to participate in the trial any futher. It was clear to me that she had no interest in the outcome of her case – she only wanted to see Charlie and to give Charlie a forum to speak.

And she was found guilty of the crime of attempted assassination of a President. Candidly, I always felt Virga had a colorable case and colorable argument, but he was essentially prevented from presenting a defense by his client's own actions and conduct. Fromme was sentenced to 34 years in prison. She wound up serving that time and was finally released in August of 2009, two years after Gerald Ford died of natural causes.

During the lead up to the trial, and the trial itself, we had courthouse artists who would sketch everyone in the courtroom. Photographs in court were not permitted, but sketch artists were acceptable. And many of them were quite good. I recall seeing quite a few sketches showing the Judge, the defendant, the attorneys, the clerk, the bailiff, the court reporter. And when they came to the two law clerks (who had chairs adjacent to the Bench) the artists invariably sketched two chairs – and nothing else. As law clerks, we were, apparently invisible.

As my two-year stint was drawing to a close in 1976, I approached a cross-roads in my life. After a successful time in law school and a prestigious appointment to a Federal clerkship, what would be my next venture? I was 29 years old.

Twenty

The Crossroads

After a Federal clerkship, I had many options available to me, especially in Sacramento. Some of the larger law firms in the area were particularly interested in me – and that was a well-trodden path by former MacBride Law Clerks, many of whom had joined those firms and had distinguished themselves in the law. That route was not for me, however. I had narrowed my options down to three. They were quite a disparate three. As my tenure wound down in 1976, I submitted a letter of application to three potential employers.

One letter was sent to Dwayne Keyes, the United States Attorney for the Eastern District of California. I had come to know Dwayne during the Fromme trial – and I had liked what I had seen. He was professional, low key, and always prepared. I thought I could learn a lot from Mr. Keyes. So, I applied to be an Assistant US Attorney, a prosecutor. At the time, that office was quite modest. Besides Mr. Keyes, there were only four or five Assistant US Attorneys. With this job I would be on the ground-floor of a very busy and fast-growing US Attorney office, working for a very competent prosecutor. It was a path that would keep me focused on Federal criminal law.

At the same time, I also submitted an application to join a brand new office that was just created by State legislation: The Office of the California State Public Defender. This office was charged with handling appellate work for indigent criminal defendants. Quinn Denvir, a defense attorney of considerable renown and experience was to be the first State Public Defender, and I thought it would be challenging and interesting to be there at the very start of this endeavor. This was a path that would find me practicing State criminal law. It was the flip side of prosecution.

Finally, I sent a letter of application to the new Governor of California, Jerry Brown, who had been sworn into office in January of 1975, following his election in 1974. I sent the letter to Jim Mulligan and Arden McConnell – two political operatives for Jerry whom I had met during the campaign in 1974. In retrospect, I was incredibly naïve to think that I could join the new Brown administration at a high level right out of the box. In my application letter I told Jim and Arden that while I would love to work in the new administration, I was only interested in a position on the Governor's Senior Staff. Quite a demand from a 29-year-old.

So, the die was (or I should say "dies") were cast. The first thing I did was take the State Public Defender test. Because this was a new civil service position in the state, I had to take a test like all the other applicants. I did pretty well, scoring 99 out of 100 possible points. But my ultimate score was listed as 104 (I received 5 extra points as a veteran's preference). Ultimately, the score of 104 was the clincher. And with that score of 104, I received the highest score in the State of California, was #1 on the list, and was offered the job as a Deputy State Public Defender.

Over the subsequent years I have often contemplated this crossroads I had reached in my life, although I didn't give it a great deal of thought at the time. I was young, ambitious, hungry for new challenges. But, in retrospect, each of these three applications, if accepted, would take me in a totally different direction with a totally different career. It was similar to the decision I had made five years earlier as to which law school I would attend. Depending on the choice, my future would have been vastly different.

So, what to choose? I had been accepted by the State Public Defender, and then within days, I heard from Dwayne Keyes, offering me a job as an Assistant United States Attorney. I had heard nothing from the Governor's Office. So, now I had to choose between two excellent paths: one on the defense side and one as a prosecutor. Ultimately, I opted to take the job with the US Attorneys Office. I decided that I would rather be on the front line as a trial attorney instead of at a desk writing appellate arguments. So, I wrote a nice thank you letter to Quinn Denvir, thanking him for the offer, but declining. And I met with Dwayne Keyes, talked about the job, worked out a starting date, and on a handshake, accepted the job of Assistant United States Attorney.

And wouldn't you know it, a day later I heard from the Governor's Office. Jim Mulligan called me and said that there was a job that might be just right for me, and it was on the Governor's senior staff working in the "Horseshoe". Let me explain the concept of the "Horseshoe". The Governor's Office is in the State Capitol Building and its configuration is that of a horseshoe surrounding a large reception area and central meeting area. The Governor has a very large staff, but only the crème de la crème have offices in the horseshoe. The rest of the staff work out of various buildings and offices throughout Sacramento. Even Jim Mulligan didn't have an office in the horseshoe. It's coveted in the political pecking order. The horseshoe is populated by the Governor, himself, his chief of staff, and key senior staff including the legislative secretary, the cabinet secretary, the press secretary, the appointments secretary, the legal secretary, and so on. The particular position that was potentially available for me was as the deputy appointments secretary. The appointments secretary and the deputy appointments secretary assist the Governor in making those thousands of non-civil service, exempt job appointments allocated to the Governor in the executive branch of government. It's a huge job, and an important one.

Well, I was facing a dilemma. I had already accepted the job with the US Attorney's Office. But, it occurred to me that I should play out the hand that I was dealt, and see where it would take me. An appointment was set for me to go into the Governor's Office to meet with the Governor regarding the position. The time of the appointment was 9 a.m. That morning I put on the best of my three suits, shined my shoes, and drove to Sacramento from Davis. I parked in the garage across the street from the State Capitol, and as is my wont, I arrived early, well before 9 a.m. I never want to be late. I checked in with the receptionist, a well-known and pleasant lady by the name of Jackie, who had worked as the receptionist for several Governors before and after Jerry Brown. She announced my presence. I didn't really think I would be ushered right in to the Governor at 9 a.m. I figured that I would have to meet at least a couple of other folks beforehand. And I did. I spent some time with Dr. Carlotta Mellon, who served as the Governor's appointments secretary. She and I were actually about the same age and we hit if off pretty well. I also met with the Governor's chief of staff (Gray Davis at the time), as well as the director of administration, and a couple of other folks on the senior staff. But by 10:30 a.m. I had met with everyone who had needed to meet with me. Except, of course, the Governor himself. I was moved to a small room near the Governor's private office, and I continued to wait. And so I waited. And waited. 11 a.m. 12 noon. 1 p.m. 2 p.m. Still waiting. 3 p.m. 4 p.m. The mind starts playing tricks at that point. One moves from irritation, to boredom, to indignation, to anger. The phlegm starts to rise. Then the bile. Who did he think he was, making me wait all this time? The appointment was for 9 a.m. wasn't it? 5 p.m. 6 p.m.

But as the hours trickled by, an interesting thing was happening. I realized that I really wanted this job with the Governor. I came to the conclusion that I would wait however long it took, because this was the path I wanted my life to take at this time. I entered a zone of tranquility. 7 p.m. 8 p.m.

And then, just before 9 p.m. (some 12 hours after the original time for the interview) Jacques Barzhagi walked into the room where I was waiting. Now, Jacques Barzhagi was a bit of a legendary character during the first administration of Jerry Brown. He was short, very trim and wiry, with sharp features and a bald head. He usually dressed all in black like a ninja. He had no defined role in the administration, but he was one of only a handful of people who could walk into the Governor's private office anytime he wanted. In Jerry Brown's first administration as Governor (let's call it Brown 1) there were only three spheres of power in that office: The Governor, of course, was the ultimate sphere of power. Gray Davis, the Governor's chief of staff, was given great authority, and was a second sphere of power. And Jacques Barzaghi, the man with no portfolio (and every portfolio), was the third sphere.

Jacques Barzaghi slipped into the small room where I was sitting (patiently by this time), and said not a word. Then he clasped his hands together as if in prayer, looked at me with his dark eyes, and said four words: "The rose is blooming." Then as noiselessly as he entered, he glided to the door and departed.

As I sat pondering this somewhat bizarre development, the Governor's personal secretary (a young lady who always looked out-of-breath and harried) came in, ushered me into the Governor's private office where I met with Governor Jerry Brown. Carlotta was in the room as well. This time the Governor didn't tell me that I looked pale. (But after a 12-hour wait I certainly would have been forgiven a little pallor.) Our conversation was brief – in fact, I don't remember any of the spoken words. But it didn't matter – the decision had already been made. The bottom line, I was offered the job of Deputy Appointments Secretary. Apparently, Carlotta had been pushing for some time to have a deputy. The job was, in reality, huge as the Governor had thousands and thousands of appointments ranging all the way from Agency Secretaries and Department Directors at one end to Fair Board Directors and Regional Water Board members at the other extreme. All were important in their own ways, and the all were exempt Governor's appointments.

I accepted the offer on the spot, and agreed to start within a very short time.

First things first, however. I had to meet with Dwayne Keyes, the U.S. Attorney to explain that I could not accept his courteous offer to serve as an Assistant United States Attorney. Mr. Keyes, ever the gentleman, was gracious in understanding, and let me go with his blessing. I imagine he had plenty of other excellent candidates as the job of an Assistant U.S. Attorney was a coveted one.

And so, my life in the political arena began in earnest in 1976. I was 29 years old. Carlotta Mellon was also 29. Gray Davis, the Chief of Staff, was 33. And Jerry Brown, the Governor, was all of 37. In retrospect, we were kids. But we had enthusiasm, energy, and ideas and we were at the very apex of California State Government.

But before I talk about my years with Governor Jerry Brown, allow me to mention a very significant event in my life that occurred in 1977. Lea and I had wanted children and we were blessed with the birth of our son, Jason, in 1971. We wanted a second child but lived through the misfortune of a miscarriage and then the death of a child who only lived for a few days. We still wanted a child, and so we decided to adopt. I learned that adoptions, in the 1970's were complex processes, particularly through adoption agencies or foreign adoptions. So, on a bit of a whim, I made a phone call to John Virga and I asked John if he had any leads to a private adoption. Much to my surprise and delight, John said he did come into contact from time to time with people who wanted to give up their newborns to private adoption. I told John we were very interested, and John responded that he would contact me the very next time he had the opportunity to facilitate a private adoption.

And John was a man of his word. In a matter of only a few weeks, I got a call from John who asked me, "What are you doing tomorrow?"

Turns out that John Virga was in touch with a young woman who was in the hospital giving birth to child and she wanted to give that child up to adoption. According to John, the woman – a tall blond lady – did not even know that she was pregnant until she started having labor pains and went to the hospital. She gave birth to a healthy baby girl and Lea and I went to the hospital to pick up the baby about two days after the birth. John prepared the papers for a private adoption, the lady signed off on them, and suddenly, Lea and I were parents again of a baby we named Janis Ellen Rosenberg. (Yes, Lea and I were heavily influenced by the 1970's and the music of Janis Joplin.) "Ellen" was Lea's middle name. And so, we were the parents of Jason, born in 1971 and Janis, born in 1977. I was very proud of my little family.

The press didn't know quite what to make of Jerry Brown.
Here is an editorial cartoon from the early 1970's.

Twenty-One

The Governor Jerry Brown Years

So, here I was in the Horseshoe, a member of the senior staff of the Governor of California.

I was given a private office – not huge, but certainly adequate – after all, I had to have a place where I could meet and interview prospective candidates for appointment. The Horseshoe was occupied by the key staff members of the Governor's Office. Moving clockwise from the reception area we found the office of the Director of Community Relations and the office of the Appointments Secretary. Next came the office of the Press Secretary and a small space for the Scheduling Secretary. The Cabinet Secretary's office was located right next to the Governor's private offices. The Governor's private offices consisted of a large room for two secretaries, an even larger room that the Governor used for meetings – dominated by a huge conference table, a small private bathroom, and then a small wood-paneled private working office for the Governor. Directly across the hall from the Governor's private offices was the office of the Chief of Staff. Moving around the corner, continuing in a clockwise direction, were the offices for the Legal Affairs Secretary and the Judicial Appointments Secretary (Tony Kline who would later become an appellate Justice held both those jobs with Governor Brown), the Legislative Secretary, and a couple of senior legislative assistants. At the next corner of the Horseshoe was the office of the Director of Administration. Turning the corner was my office and also the offices for some members of the appointments staff, and then several smaller offices for Deputy Legislative Secretaries and some scheduling assistants. And that brought us back to the reception area.

I didn't know it at the time, but I would spend a total of five and one-half years working for Jerry Brown through two of his terms. The first four years were spent as the Deputy Appointments Secretary, and the last year and one-half were spent as Gray Davis' assistant, with the title of Deputy Executive Secretary and Chief of Staff.

Those four years as Deputy Appointments Secretary was a time of general drudgery, interspersed with occasional high points of great drama. I certainly paid my dues. Carlotta and I divided the workload. She, of course, kept the major appointments, and I had everything else – so, she took the quality and I got the quantity. I did not begrudge her this, because she was the Appointments Secretary and I was the Deputy – had our roles been reversed, I would have done precisely the same. Plus, I didn't mind a bit. Carlotta and I had a cordial and professional working relationship, and I operated with great independence. I had a list of boards, commissions, and committees and set about the task of finding appropriate candidates to fill the positions. Of course, most positons were filled with appointees of the prior Governor (a Republican) who would continue to serve until reappointed or replaced. With rare exceptions, California had a political history of electing Governors of both parties, often alternating between Republican and Democrat. And the new Governor of the opposite party tended to replace the prior Governor's appointees when given the opportunity. And it was no different with the Brown administration.

I had a remarkably broad portfolio of boards, commissions and committees including those involved in medicine, water, air, professions (such as dentists, nurses, optometrists, auto repair shops, etc.), local fair boards, and more. Thousands, in fact. I didn't mind. It gave me a great education in the width and depth of California state government. I even reached down into county government from time to time. When there is a vacancy on a county Board of Supervisors, it is the Governor who fills that vacancy. I had that responsibility as well, so I got quite a glimpse of county government (which served me very well many years later when I, myself, was elected to a county Board of Supervisors).

I had to "vet" the candidates to make sure they were qualified, to ensure that there were no skeletons in their closets or conflicts in their past associations that could come back to bite us, and I had to make sure they would be in tune with the Governor's philosophy of clean government and reform. From time to time, I would try to bring in folks who had helped and supported the Governor in his election. Most of my work was accomplished in my office with phone calls and interviews. I also traveled a bit. About once a month I would go to the Governor's Los Angeles Office to interview candidates, and on occasion I would go to the Governor's San Francisco Office to do the same. The Los Angeles Office had a small staff and they were always glad to see someone from the Horseshoe. The San Francisco Office, on the other hand, had no staff and the office was generally vacant – but I had a key.

The biggest single challenge that Carlotta and I faced was actual face time with the Governor. That, frankly, was a challenge for everyone in the Horseshoe. The only people in the Horseshoe who could just "walk in" to the Governor's private office at any time were Gray Davis, Jacques Barzaghi, and Tony Kline. Everyone else needed to ask for time (usually through Gray). And time was very, very hard to obtain. If Carlotta and I were lucky, we would see the Governor to talk appointments about once a month. And we had to be ready at any time of the night and day to have that meeting. Governor Brown did not keep normal 8 to 5 hours. Far from it. He might come into the office at 11 a.m. but might work till 10 or 11 at night. He would work on weekends. Sometimes we would meet him in his car – trying to discuss appointments on the fly. I remember talking about appointments with him on a commercial airplane. As time went on, however, the Governor would defer authority on appointments to Gray Davis – giving him more and more say-so on lower level positions which he could "approve" on behalf of the Governor. So, over time, I got to know Gray Davis better and better, and we got along.

There were three types of people who worked in the Governor's Office. First, there were a number of professionals who were non-political and who wound up working for Governor after Governor, regardless of party. These were all people who were experts in their fields. One of these professionals was Bob Williams who was a legislative expert – Bob knew the process of the State Senate and the State Assembly inside and out – he was a great resource to the Governor and staff and he had a private office right in the Horseshoe. Most of the other folks in the Horseshoe (the secretaries and assistants) were also non-political experts carried from administration to administration. One of these was Susie Pritchard who worked for me in Appointments – Susie was an expert in the entire appointments process. The second category of people were political appointees who were highly organized button-down-collar administrators who would move the ball from point A to point B. These were people like Gray Davis, Tony Kline and myself. The third category again included political appointees who were dreamers and thinkers and were as far from the category of "administrators" as one could imagine. The prime representative of this group was Jacques Barzaghi. Governor Brown enabled both of these latter two groups to function in his office, but there was clearly a background conflict between the Gray Davis group and the Jacques Barzaghi group. This dynamic and friction personified the Jerry Brown administration.

In truth, however, both groups were necessary to the unique Governor that was Jerry Brown. We needed the thinkers and the dreamers to come up with big ideas regarding the environment, water, air, transportation, consumer affairs, and the like. But we also needed the button-down types to bring a dose of reality to the discussion, and to plan how to implement the big ideas. Jerry was noted for challenging the status quo and bringing in people to his administration who used to be on the outside of the traditional ruling class. For example, Jerry brought in Ed Roberts, a quadriplegic, to run the Department of Rehabilitation. He brought in Adrianna Gianturco, an advocate for public transportation, to run the Department of Transportation. He brought in Richard Spohn, a public advocate, to run the Department of Consumer Affairs. Each of these people shook things up and changed the outlook of these departments. And Jerry did this up and down the line.

He also shook things up by bringing in far more women and people of color than any prior administration. Jerry Brown really opened up California state government to the tapestry of this state – men and women of all hues and ethnicities, all genders and gender identities – well before it was politically correct to do so.

And, frankly, I am very proud of my role, as Deputy Appointments Secretary, in breaking down the barriers at all levels for people who had been essentially kept out of state government since the inception of statehood in 1850. California is an incredibly diverse state. Jerry Brown made state government far more diverse than it had ever been. It was not an easy task. There was pushback at all levels. Perhaps the most notable example of this pushback is Jerry Brown's appointment of Rose Bird, a very talented woman, not only to be the first woman on the California Supreme Court, but in a dramatic statement, to be the first female Chief Justice. The forces of conservatism had their ultimate victory, however, when this talented Chief Justice was recalled after a particularly nasty campaign against her. In spite of the pushback, Jerry Brown persevered. He brought in great and diverse talent to top positions in the administration. These included Mario Obledo, a legendary leader in the Hispanic community, to serve as Secretary of the Health and Human Services Agency; Alice Lytle and Percy Pinckney, respected leaders in the Black community, as Secretary of the State and Consumer Services Agency and as Director of Community Relations, respectively, and many others from the ethnic pool of talent that composed California.

During the four years I worked as the Deputy in Appointments, much of what I did was routine, and often mundane. But there is one incident that stands out in my mind, although virtually no one is aware of it or remembers it. It concerns Jim Jones, the charismatic preacher and leader of the People's Temple. In the 1970's he was on everyone's short list of important people in San Francisco. Local political leaders tapped Jim Jones to serve on all sorts of boards and task forces. At the time, no one knew of his megalomania, let alone his insanity. This was all before he moved to a jungle commune at Jonestown, Guyana. Jones was well-connected and one day, Governor Brown signed a commission appointing Jim Jones to an important board in the criminal justice area. For some reason which I couldn't really articulate at the time, I had a bad taste in my mouth about Jones, and I held onto that commission – never released it for processing or a press release. And while I was holding that commission, the news hit that Jones' followers in Guyana had committed mass suicide, as did Jones with a bullet to his head. That commission never saw the light of day.

In 1980 my life in the Governor's Office took a rather unexpected and dramatic turn. Jerry was a proponent of "less is more" and the Governor's Office staff reflected than philosophy. He had fewer folks on his staff than previous Governors. A number of folks on Jerry's staff complained about this and sought to have help, which Jerry generally discouraged. Ultimately, some members prevailed in their quest for deputies – one example is Carlotta Mellon's request for a deputy which ultimately resulted in me joining the staff. Well, even Gray Davis decided he needed a deputy. And he certainly did. The Governor, over the years, gave Gray more and more responsibility and more and more authority to make decisions for the Governor and to speak for the Governor in a wide range of areas including legislation, appointments, community relations, press, and more. There were often more demands on Gray's time than on Jerry's time. Everyone wanted to meet with Gray and talk to Gray. And so, Gray decided he needed a deputy.

I was tapped for the job. Gray met with me and asked if I would take the job of his deputy. I was floored. But not so floored that I wouldn't accept. Of course I accepted. Gray said that he needed someone to take the load off him, and immediately handed me a list of over 20 high-powered and high-ranking folks who wanted to meet with Gray – he asked me to meet with them on his behalf. He then gave me a list of some 50 people who had called him – and asked me to call them back on his behalf and "handle it." Gray's official title in the office was Executive Secretary and Chief of Staff. I assumed that my title would simply be Deputy Chief of Staff. But Gray insisted that my title would be Deputy Executive Secretary and Chief of Staff. He wanted my title to have enough panache that people who talked to me would feel that they were communicating with someone in the very top echelon. Jerry Brown's office had never had a deputy chief of staff. That title, however, had long been used by previous governors. Governor Ronald Reagan, in fact, had had a very powerful deputy chief of staff in the person of Michael Deaver who at the time, was considered one of the governor's very top assistants. In addition to the title, Gray carved out an office for me, immediately next door to his and across the hall from the Governor's private office. We shared Gray's two secretaries – which caused a bit of quiet resentment at first – but that soon dissipated when the secretaries saw that I was actually taking a significant workload from Gray's shoulders and also took a burden off them – they didn't have to constantly say "we'll get back to you."

So, in 1980 I assumed the title of Deputy Executive Secretary and Chief of Staff, and now my portfolio was as broad as it can be in the Governor's Office. The job was interesting, fast-paced, and at times, exhausting. But I was young and loving it. Interestingly, very soon after Gray brought me in as his deputy, Jacques Barzaghi made a pitch to the Governor for a title and a deputy. Jacques – who had no portfolio – now became the Cabinet Secretary and took over that office. Jacques also insisted that he needed a deputy as well. Jacques got his wish and hired a young man by the name of Rosenblum. If Gray had a Rosenberg, Jacques was going to have a Rosenblum. In a way, it was humorous. And, in the end Rosenberg and Rosenblum got along just fine.

I served as Deputy Chief of Staff for a year and a half out of my five and a half years working for Jerry Brown. That year and a half was an amazing interlude. I had meetings regularly with State Senators and Assemblymen, County Supervisors and Mayors, leaders of business and labor, political contributors, lobbyists of all kinds, and many other leading citizens. Those contacts served me well for many, many years after my time with Governor Brown.

But the time was running out. Jerry had been elected Governor in 1974 and was sworn into office at the start of 1975. I joined the administration late – in 1976. Jerry was re-elected in 1978, and started his second term as Governor at the start of 1979. The second term would wrap up at the end of 1982. I decided to depart in 1981. I left a bit early, on very good terms with everyone in the administration. I was 35 years old in 1981, and I felt it was time to go (the administration of Governor Jerry Brown would all end in 1982 anyway and everyone had to find a new home in any event). I was trained as a lawyer and I had a sense that it was time for me to practice law. So, with a series of cordial goodbyes to my friends and colleagues in the administration of Governor Jerry Brown, I started practicing law – a career that would span the next 20 years.

A rare photo of Governor Jerry Brown with his senior staff and support staff from the Horseshoe. There I am in the front row, second from the right.

Twenty-Two

Life as a Lawyer

I had graduated from law school in 1974, but didn't start practicing law until seven years later, in 1981. I became a rookie lawyer at the age of 35. Interestingly enough, in all my years of practicing law, I never served as an associate attorney – I was always a partner. That's unusual, but my background gave me the contacts to make that happen.

Every part of my life, I have found, served as a stepping stone to the next part of my life. My entry into the practice of law was no different.

Ever since I worked with Steve Felderstein as law clerks for Chief Judge Tom MacBride, we stayed in touch as friends. We worked in the same town – Sacramento – and would often meet for lunch. In my work for Governor Brown, I even facilitated an appointment for Steve on the California Health Facilities Commission, a relatively interesting and prestigious government commission, which Steve thoroughly enjoyed. Steve had left the law clerking one year before I did. He went directly into the practice of law, joining as an associate to a solo practitioner. While working for this attorney, the president of the Sacramento Gold soccer team came to see the firm because the team was in financial trouble and needed protection in Federal Bankruptcy Court. The solo practitioner knew nothing about bankruptcy law and sent the case to Steve. Coincidentally, the Federal Bankruptcy Act, at that very moment in time, had undergone a complete overhaul, and Steve became as knowledgeable in the new law as anyone else in town. He took the case and learned all about the bankruptcy code. Over time, Steve developed into one of the premier bankruptcy lawyers in Sacramento, specializing in Chapter 11 workouts. There was a lot of demand for bankruptcy lawyers, and Steve soon took on a bright young associate by the name of Mike McManus. Their law practice flourished. Over the years I was working for Jerry Brown, Steve often would encourage me, over lunch, to join him in the practice of law.

In 1981 I made that leap and agreed to join him. Steve was ready to make a change in his practice as well, to elevate Mike McManus to partnership status. And thus was born the law firm of Felderstein, Rosenberg and McManus. Steve had a law office in Downtown Sacramento at 455 Capitol Mall – a prestigious address. Seems like I was perennially located on the Capitol Mall, whether it be with the Federal court, State government, or the private practice of law. The physical office space was, however, rather small for a law firm. I recall my first office was literally a converted telephone switching room, with a lot of circuits that made a lot of noise. In the beginning, there was just four of us: Steve, myself, Mike, and Pam, the office manager – essentially a Girl Friday who also did para-legal work. We were a happy group, and soon moved to newer and better offices – a few blocks off Capitol Mall, but still in downtown Sacramento. Steve and Mike continued their work in bankruptcy which was a growing and lucrative practice. I intended to develop a practice as a civil litigator. Steve and Mike sent me some work to the extent they needed help in civil litigation. And then, one day soon after I joined them, a big client walked through my door into my little switching room.

I had received a phone call from Jim Mulligan, the gentleman I had worked with years ago on the Jerry Brown campaign. Jim was working as a lobbyist for caregivers in the developmental disability world. Developmental disabilities are conditions that cover a wide range of permanent disabilities that occur in the human body at a very early age (certainly before the age of 17) and present a life-long condition. The disabilities include mental retardation, epilepsy, cerebral palsy, spina bifida, and other conditions. I had acquired some knowledge of the world of developmental disabilities during my Jerry Brown years, when I assisted the Governor in making appointments to the State Developmental Disabilities Board and regional boards that deal with developmental disabilities. The State of California, at the time, had a Department of Developmental Services Tom McClintock, as well as a series of Regional Centers, throughout California, that provided services to persons with developmental disabilities. The state even had Developmental Centers which were, in effect, state hospitals for the most severe cases. Over the years, however, and particularly during the terms of Governor Ronald Reagan, there was an effort to empty the state hospitals serving persons with developmental disabilities and move them into the community. This was primarily driven in an effort to save the state money, not for some altruistic purpose. They did, in fact, virtually empty out the state hospitals but local community services were not commensurate with the needs of this population, particularly the most severe cases.

Jim and I had always gotten along quite well in an easy friendship. Now, he needed a lawyer. Jerry Brown was still the Governor (for one more year) so the perception was that I had some connections to people in authority. He knew I had some knowledge about the subject, and frankly, there was no attorney in California who specialized in this area of the law. He asked for my help on a problem he was having with the Department of Developmental Disabilities and with Regional Centers – and he needed legal help. Jim represented CALARF – the California Association of Rehabilitation Facilities. Other than for the most acute cases in state developmental centers (state hospitals), the state did not provide direct services to people with developmental disabilities. Nor did the Regional Centers – the Regional Centers determined if people were qualified to receive services, and then worked with the developmentally disabled person (and that person's parents or relatives) to find appropriate services in the community. That's where CALARF came into play. CALARF was, essentially, the trade organization on behalf of service providers throughout California. These service providers ran the gamut from mom-and-pop facilities to large corporate service providers. There was a great deal of money in the system because developmental disabilities were quite prevalent, and they were quite permanent – there is no "cure" for developmental disabilities – once a person has them, they have them for a lifetime.

The problem that Jim brought to my attention was the following: In what appeared to me to be a rather transparent attempt to save money, Regional Centers which determined that people in their jurisdiction were eligible for services would not arrange those services immediately. Instead, Regional Centers would place these eligible people on "waiting lists" – sometimes for months and months – before services would be provided. This was causing impacts on eligible people, their families, and service providers.

It didn't take me long to conclude that this was not right. So, I took the case and went about doing research. I discovered the Lanterman Act. A far-sighted legislator by the name of Frank Lanterman had written a statute – eventually passed by the Legislature and signed into law by the Governor – which laid out the services that should be available for persons with developmental disabilities. This law came to be known as the Lanterman Act. In reviewing this statute, I came to the conclusion that we could use this act as the leverage we needed to blow up the waiting lists.

Soon after CALARF retained me, they were joined by ARC-California – the Association for Retarded Citizens – California. This was the association of recipients of services, composed of persons with mental retardation, parents, and professionals in the field. I now had a coalition behind me.

The first thing I did is to schedule meetings with the Director of Developmental Services – the department of state government which was responsible for programs and services in this area. I knew the Director from my prior work for Jerry Brown. The meetings I had were very cordial, but not very productive. The Director simply bounced the ball back to the Regional Centers, saying it was the Regional Centers that imposed the waiting lists, not the Department. I then met with the leaders of Regional Centers – this was challenging as there were several such centers in California, each assigned to a different region of the state, with different leadership and acting with autonomy from each other. The Regional

Centers argued, with a straight face, that they had no waiting lists. Without question, they did. They also argued that even if they had waiting lists, such waiting lists were necessitated by the volume of demand for services.

The bottom line is that I became convinced that no change would occur from within. If we were going to change the system, it would have to happen through the courts. I had many meetings throughout the state with representatives of CALARF and ARC-California. Needless to say, filing a lawsuit against the very people that feed your program is a pretty large hurdle. But ultimately, my clients became convinced that the waiting lists were intolerable, particularly for the folks who needed services, and they authorized the lawsuit.

So, I unleashed the dogs of litigation. Two things happened. First, I was successful beyond expectations. I argued the case through the trial court, to the court of appeals, and ultimately to the California Supreme Court. The case was called ARC-California vs. State of California, and it made new law. My case determined that persons with developmental disabilities – be they mental retardation, cerebral palsy, epilepsy, autism, and other such disabilities – had the right to services and could not be placed on waiting lists to languish waiting for those services. It was a huge and seminal victory. Second, I instantly became the leading lawyer in California on the issue of developmental disabilities law. Advocates, parents of developmentally disabled persons, providers of services all beat a path to my law firm door – dozens of cases, year after year, came my way. And I was remarkably successful in suing the State of California and Regional Centers on a wide range of issues. Further, the word got out, and other advocates for disabled citizens (like the blind) came to see me. This one case opened up a remarkable career in the law, that lasted for two decades. In fact, when I became a Judge in 2003, I turned my practice over to my associate at the time, Chad Carlock, who continued representing clients in this field for another two decades – it became the foundation of his law practice.

My career practicing law spanned close to 20 years and only

ended when I became a Judge. It encompassed three phases.

The first phase was the small law firm of Felderstein Rosenberg and McManus which we founded in 1981. We were a congenial group, with a prosperous firm and a solid practice. In fact, in the span of about five years our little firm grew from three lawyers to eight lawyers, before we entered the second phase. Our little firm had a lot of collegiality and spirit, and even had a softball team called "The McFelderbergs".

That second phase encompassed the years 1986 to 1996. In 1986, the Felderstein Rosenberg firm merged with the most prestigious, oldest, and largest firm in Sacramento: Diepenbrock, Wulff, Plant & Hannegan. Diepenbrock was the old line firm in Sacramento – well known, well-connected, and well-staffed with top-notch lawyers covering almost all practice areas. At the time, the Diepenbrock firm had over 40 lawyers. When we joined in the merger, we created a large firm of over 50 lawyers. It was an interesting cultural mix. The Diepenbrock firm was composed primarily of Republican lawyers (in fact, Dan Lungren, joined the firm for awhile and I worked with him – he was the Republican candidate for Governor). The Felderstein Rosenberg firm was primarily Democrats. But we really never talked politics in the office and the merger was successful. Steve, Mike and I all came in as partners in the new merged firm. Steve was so well-respected that in a few years he became the managing partner of the merged firm. The Diepenbrock firm had offices on Capitol Mall. I was actually quite happy in the practice of law during this time, and I made a great deal of money during those ten years with the large firm. As an added bonus, I was still able to be involved in politics during these years. State government during this period was under the control of Republican governors, so I focused on local politics in my community of Davis California. I was very happy being able to live in two worlds: law and local politics. I will dedicate a chapter of this memoir to my time in local elected office.

The third phase of my career in law started in 1996 and ended with my appointment as a Judge of the Superior Court in 2003. In 1996 I was elected as a Yolo County Supervisor. There are five

Supervisors in every county of California (with the exception of the City and County of San Francisco which had a greater number as a combined city and county). Each Supervisor represents a large geographic district of the county. It is structured to be a full-time or nearly full-time endeavor. Having been elected to the Board of Supervisors, I decided that I could not make that daily commute from Davis to Sacramento, and dedicate the time to a full-time practice in a large law firm. With gratitude, I said good-bye to Diepenbrock, Wulff, Plant & Hannegan and opened my own little law office in Downtown Davis – the Law Offices of Dave Rosenberg. I figured that I could continue a modicum of a law practice – completely under my control and not answerable to law partners – while serving as a County Supervisor. It was one of the best decisions I ever made in my life.

I loved my little law office. I rented an office from Dan Dowling who ran his real estate office from an old house at the corner of 3rd and D Streets. Rent was cheap. I was answerable only to myself. I could come and go as I pleased. I had plenty of time to attend to my County Supervisor duties, and I could pick and choose my clients. Much to my surprise, however, I found that I was making the same level of income as I had been making in the big firm – the result of low overhead. I had very few expenses other than rent. I did my own typing (I was, after all, a trained journalist), and when I needed major jobs typed, I tapped into a young woman who lived in Davis raising her child who worked from home and needed some extra income. I developed a good-sized clientele representing agencies with disputes against the State of California, and became quite adept in administrative law. I also picked up the occasional local client who needed some property work, or a contract, or a will. It was the best of all worlds as a lawyer. In fact, I got so busy that I had to hire an associate to help out, and eventually even hired a paralegal. The associate was a bright young lawyer named Chad Carlock. I created a structure so that I could pay him a living wage. He worked in my law practice and I paid him a salary. I also hired him as my deputy in my county supervisor office – that position was not a full-time job, but between the law firm and the supervisor work, Chad had a full-time job and a decent salary. Eventually, in 2003 when the Governor appointed me to be a Judge, I just gave my law practice to Chad, without charge, and he has made a good living from that practice and raised a fine family.

The paralegal story is an interesting one. For decades, the leading columnist in Davis has been Bob Dunning. His columns were ubiquitous, humorous, and often sarcastic. Everyone reads Bob's daily columns. He is like the Herb Cain of the community. Turns out that during my years on the Davis City Council and as Mayor and County Supervisor, I was one of Bob's regular and featured targets. The impression was that I was Bob's bete noire. But in reality we used each other – I was grist for his daily column, and he gave me the publicity and attention that every public official secretly desires. We were actually the best of enemies. Well, one day, out of the blue, Bob called me on the phone. He needed a lawyer.

In addition to his work for the Davis Enterprise, Bob had been hired by a radio station in Sacramento and had his own show on the air. That day, however, they had told him he was being terminated. I told Bob to stand by – I was driving over to pick him up and we were going to Sacramento. I did just that. Ironically for Bob, I drove over in my black Cadillac, a favorite foil for Bob's chiding. I picked Bob up at his house, we drove in to Sacramento, walked into the studio and I asked to see the general manager. Bob waited outside the office. I introduced myself as Bob's lawyer and we had a heart-to-heart chat. Bottom line, they agreed that day to pay Bob a significant severance package. Needless to say, after that day Bob and I had a much different relationship.

In fact, to tide Bob over I offered to hire him as a paralegal. Bob was actually legally trained. He had graduated from King Hall at UCD in 1973 – one year before I graduated. But he had never taken the bar exam – so he could not practice as a lawyer. Bob worked for me for a couple of years and he was a valuable resource for my little law office. I used Bob as a fact-finder and researcher, and he was top–notch. I often sent Bob on trips to clients to get the facts and information on the ground, from El Centro to Chico. Clients loved him, and he always gave me thorough reports. He was, after all, a gifted writer.

In retrospect, of my three law firms – my sole practice at the Law Offices of Dave Rosenberg was the best. It was almost idyllic. As noted, I could set my own hours and work as long and as hard as I wanted, or play hooky for the day if I wanted. I enjoyed the camaraderie with Chad and Bob, and I valued my clients. I was doing important work for them, and helping to shape law for those who were disabled. It gave me great satisfaction to help my clients, and it was always a wonder to me when I opened my mail and saw a check payable to my law firm.

But if there is one constant in my life, it is the fact that I never really did one thing at a time. I was like the one-man band, simultaneously plunking the banjo, blowing on the harmonica, jangling the bells on my ankles, and knocking the cymbals on my knees together.

I handled some high profile cases in my law practice which were reported in the press from time to time.

Twenty-Three

Local Elected Office Beckons

Local government held an allure for me for some reason.

I guess part of it is that I enjoy problem solving. In life it's good to know your skills and your deficits. Math may be a deficit for me, but identifying a problem and coming up with a solution is a skill. And so, local government provided an opportunity to put my skill to use to help other people and to make my community a better place. Well, Davis, California had become "my community" when I moved there with my family in 1971. My first foray into local government saw me applying for a seat on a local government commission in 1980. I applied for an open seat on the City of Davis Planning Commission. I was pretty naïve about local government in those days. I learned years later that the Planning Commission is the crème de la crème of local boards and commissions, and folks don't get appointed to those slots unless they were heavily involved in the campaigns of a sitting member of the City Council. And the Planning Commission is viewed as a stepping stone to the City Council. Certainly no one is going to get appointed to the Planning Commission who might pose a "threat" as a future competitor to sitting Council members. I didn't get the appointment, but I did get 2 votes from the 5 City Council members.

Encouraged, I applied for a lesser board, and was ultimately appointed to the City's Historical Resources Commission, charged with overseeing and protecting the City's designated historical resources and buildings. My first active involvement in city politics was a forceful effort to save the historic old City Library building, which was destined to be torn down to make way for a parking structure. I lobbied hard with other citizens, and we were successful in saving the old library. We convinced the City Council to not tear it down, but rather to move it to a corner in the Central Park. The day the trucks lined up to move that building was a day of satisfaction to me. It was quite a project, lifting that building up, moving it over city streets, lifting telephone wires, turning corners, and setting it down in the park. And the building now sits, restored, in Central Park functioning as the City of Davis Museum. It's called the Hattie Weber Building, named after the city's first librarian.

With a taste for local government on my tongue, I decided to jump in with both feet. I announced my campaign for the Davis City Council election of 1982. (So, clearly, the fears of some council members were true, that appointing me to the Planning Commission would simply enable a future competitor for the council.) Council members in Davis were elected to four-year terms. Davis held a council election every two years. In one cycle two council members were elected and in the next cycle three council members were elected. I built up a small campaign staff, took the obligatory photos of myself and my family, created some brochures, and prepared to be a candidate for local elected office.

Even though I was relatively new in town, I reckoned that I had a decent chance. One of the two incumbents had announced that he would not run for re-election, and the other incumbent who had already served two terms on the Council, after much hemming and hawing, also announced he would not run again. The hemming-and-hawing councilman's name was Tom Tomasi and he personally told me he would not run. So it looked like two seats were wide open – a rare event in Davis politics which typically generates lots of candidates for the council races. One candidate for office in 1982 was Ann Evans, a young energetic woman who was known as an environmentalist and was one of the founders of the Davis Food Coop. To me, she looked like the odds-on favorite to win a seat. I thought that with hard-campaigning I could snag that other seat.

Then, on literally the last day to file, Tom changed his mind and decided he would run again for a third term. It was a stunner and a bit of a double-cross in my book. A number of people told me to drop out. But I didn't. I had made a decision, and as is my style, I stuck with it. Ultimately, there were eight candidates who filed for the two seats. The way it worked in Davis back in those days is that the top two vote-getters are elected – there are no run-offs. And it was a city-wide election. In 1982, there were no districts – all members of the City Council were elected by all the people who lived in Davis.

Running for local office was exhilarating and fun for me. The only person who enjoyed it more seemed to be my wife, Lea. She took to campaigning like a duck to water. We walked, I believe, the entire town of Davis, and knocked on a great number of doors talking to voters. The campaign process was educational. Both Lea and I certainly learned a lot. In the end, I did not win a seat on the council in 1982. We were electing two; I came in a third place in the field of eight. As I predicted, Ann took first place, Tom came in second, and I was a respectable third. The 1982 campaign had certainly taught me a great deal about local politics and the Davis political scene. It also gave me good name recognition. I had run a solid campaign. It was also a positive campaign – I never went negative. My showing throughout the city was so solid, in fact, that I was encouraged by many folks to run again.

And so, I did. In the very next City Council election in 1984, I was a candidate. In that year there were three seats up for election, but there was a huge field of twelve candidates. Same hard campaigning, walking the precincts, doing small fundraiser events, going to forums and giving speeches. Because of my name identification, I was considered a favorite in this election and it showed. Other candidates often copied what I said, which only reinforced my standing.

This time I won. I came in as the second-highest vote getter and was elected to the Davis City Council in 1984. You have to have a thick epidermis to be in politics, whether it is at the local, state or national level. My skin is thick. I subscribe to the statement that former South Carolina Governor Mark Sanford once uttered: "I think the fatal flaw of a lot of people in politics is that they want to be loved." I never suffered that flaw. I knew my worth. I knew what I wanted to do and I knew how to get there. I also realized that everyone in the business of politics and government will be despised by some. So be it. I can handle it.

So, in 1984, at the age of 38, the little immigrant boy from Germany was an elected official in California. I had come a long way from that little village in Bavaria. But as is my wont in life, I never did one thing at a time.

In 1985, at the age of 39, I did something I'd never done before. I don't do normal hobbies (like golf, bowling, or tennis). In 1985 – notwithstanding all the engagements I had with my family, my law practice, my city council position – I decided to write a novel. It became kind of a hobby or avocation for me. Frankly, I did it primarily to prove to myself that I had the discipline to accomplish the task. Writing a novel is all about discipline and perseverance. The genre I chose was science fiction, in part because I enjoyed reading science fiction (when I had the time to read), but mainly because "anything goes" in science fiction – there are really no boundaries. I set about the task and resolved that I would write every single day. And I did. I had a daily goal of a certain number of pages, and I remember meeting the goal each day. I found writing to be both challenging and stimulating. The most interesting thing I discovered while writing the book is that the book, at times, wrote itself. That is to say, that I remember typing a scene, getting into the scene, and saying to myself, "Gee, I can't wait to see what happens next." In any event, the "next" took care of itself and I finished writing the book in a bit over six months. I titled it "Endgame" and had it published in 1986. The book was a tale of two civilizations that lived together on a fictional planet. These civilizations had been engaged in a trench war for so long that the reason for the war had been lost in time – the war had become the basis of their existence. The gravamen of the book was all about a third force (with adherents on both sides of the trenches) who were trying to end the conflict. It was never a best-seller because I had no agent and had to self-publish. But I wrote the book not to make money or become famous – but rather to see if I could do it. Much like the mountain climber who was asked why he climbed that mountain who responded, "Because it is there."

So, back to the city council. There followed a second campaign in 1988 where I was re-elected and wound up serving a second term, and then a third campaign in 1992 where I was re-elected to serve a third term. In the history of the City of Davis, very few Council members get to serve three terms.

In those days, Council member selected the Mayor, and I was elected Mayor by my council colleagues in 1986 and then again in 1994 – each time serving a two-year term as the Mayor of Davis. Council members were also elected citywide, not just representing a district composed of one-fifth of the city.

I served twelve years (three terms) on the Davis City, and four of those years I served as Mayor. I thoroughly enjoyed my time on the City Council and as Mayor. The Council was generally divided between moderates and progressives (with an occasional conservative thrown in for good measure). I tended to straddle both the moderate and progressive wings, and so I wound up in the majority during virtually my entire tenure. Over several years, I was part of a majority known as "The Gang of Three" – composed of Ann Evans, Mike Corbett, and myself. Because we were a solid majority, we could enact whatever plan we felt was best for the city.

My main goals were slowing growth, preserving the surrounding farmland and creating a strong downtown shopping area. I was quite successful in all three areas. Of course, we had our social issues to deal with (like declaring Davis a nuclear-free zone) but I found that city government is generally focused on planning and building issues – the social issues were more in the wheelhouse of the County Board of Supervisors.

Service on the City Council was another building block in my life, and an important one. It opened many doors for me. One such door involved Rush Limbaugh. The other door was the creation of "Rosenberg's Rules of Order". The third door was my election to the Yolo County Board of Supervisors.

How does Rush Limbaugh come into the picture? Well, it

happened in 1987. In the late 1980's Rush Limbaugh was a big deal in the Sacramento region. This is where he started with a conservative radio talk show before he moved to the big time in New York City. But in 1987 he was without question the best-known showman in Sacramento. Channel 13 – the local ABC television affiliate – was in the process of offering Limbaugh time on television – his first breakout from radio to TV. The concept was to have a live, unscripted and unrehearsed "debate" as a segment of their evening news. It was going to be called "At Odds". The station had signed up Limbaugh to be the conservative voice in that debate format. There was only one problem. They had no liberal voice. Coincidentally, one of my law office clients was Channel 13 and the general manager of that station knew that I was serving as Mayor of Davis. In those days, Davis was referred to as the "People's Republic of Davis" – based on a perception (generally true) that we were a liberal and progressive university town. Perception is all you need in television and the general manager asked me to be the liberal voice on "At Odds."

I thought it would be a hoot, and I readily agreed to be part of the debate. What followed was a one-year stint on live television. Twice a week, Limbaugh and I would head to the studio to lock horns in a debate on a current politically or socially charged issue. The news anchors would throw the subject out to the two of us like a cut of red meat – and as noted we did it live, without scripts or rehearsals. It was basically, "Rush and Dave – what do you think of that anti-abortion bill pending a vote in Georgia?" And, for the next five minutes, Rush and Dave would have at it. It was fun, exhilarating, it helped me to think on my feet (even though we were seated), and it certainly refined my skills as a debater and orator. It brought me considerable local visibility. I learned that the medium of television is incredibly powerful. We were even featured in TV Guide at one time.

I'm often asked about Limbaugh. I can't say much. We never agreed on anything. We never went out for a drink after the show, and we certainly never became friends. He seemed very one-dimensional to me. I viewed him as a consummate professional – he was always honing his skills and techniques as a speaker and debater. After the debate, the viewers could actually "vote" by dialing a phone number on who they agreed with, Rush or Dave. Based on Rush's local following – he normally "won" the debates based on these phone votes. But I held my own. "At Odds" was rather popular, and after a year of these debates, the station wanted to crank it up to three or four debates every week. That was just too much for me, plus Rush was on his way to the Big Apple and a national audience. I enjoyed myself, learned a lot, and got to tell Rush Limbaugh, on a regular basis, that he was full of it. What's not to like.

Another offspring from my years on the Davis City Council was the development and publication of "Rosenberg's Rules of Order." This is a set of rules of parliamentary procedure, that have become so popular that they are now used by hundreds and hundreds of city councils, boards of supervisors, planning commissions, boards, commissions, committees, corporations, private clubs and others throughout the United States. I did not set out to write such a set of rules nor to come to be known as an expert in parliamentary procedure, but it all happened in a back-door kind of way. It started during my first term as Mayor on the Davis City Council. One of my goals was to make sure that all the many boards and commissions in Davis (and there were a lot of them) operated transparently and were user-friendly to the public. So, one day I invited all the chairs and vice-chairs of our boards and commissions to meet with me, as Mayor, to talk about how we could and should interact with the public. There was a rather good turnout – it appeared that no Mayor had ever previously gathered all the chairs and vice-chairs for a chit-chat. I proceeded to explain my goal to make sure we operated transparently and that the public was fully engaged and informed about our processes and our actions. I explained the basics of parliamentary procedure: motions, amendments, substitute motions, discussion protocol, reconsideration, motions to limit debate, motions to table, etc. I put all this in the simplest possible terms. It was my belief that there are three types of people who attend public meetings: those who know the rules, those who think they know the rules and those who don't know the rules. It was my further belief that if everyone actually knows the rules, then everyone is on a level playing field – and the folks who know the rules or who think they know the rules can't bully those who don't. But to accomplish that – the rules had to be available, simple and understandable.

The "bible" of parliamentary procedure is "Robert's Rules of Order", a treatise developed by a military officer in 1876. It is a very detailed and complex tome, routinely adopted by public bodies, that virtually no one has actually read. It is an excellent body of work – if you are a member of a parliament, but it is way too complex for a city council or board of supervisors or planning commission or club. So, my goal was to simplify. I explained a set of rules that was not in conflict with Robert's, but was much pared down – yet covered 99% of what a small body would need.

Well, my presentation was a hit, so I decided to do it again the very next year. To my surprise, the Davis chairs and vice chairs invited their counterparts from other communities in Yolo County – Woodland, West Sacramento, and Winters – as well as some boards and commissions from nearby cities in other counties. Suddenly, I had over 50 people in the audience. And, once again, it was a hit. In the third year, I was asked to teach this "course" on parliamentary procedure once again, but as it turned out I had another engagement so I took my notes and put them in the form of a treatise. That was handed out to the participants.

And thus was born "Rosenberg's Rules of Order."

I subsequently presented lectures on these rules to gatherings of the League of California Cities and the County Supervisors Association, and to lots of regional groups. The League eventually put the rules in a booklet form, but that was really unnecessary as you can download them from the Internet anytime you want. Just go to Google or any other search engine and type in Rosenberg's Rules of Order and voila – they are yours. And while it took Robert's Rules of Order over 50 years to permeate the public consciousness, with the speed of the Internet, it took Rosenberg's Rules of Order less than 5 years to become ubiquitous. Much to my amazement, my rules have become popular because of their simplicity (you can read and understand them in less than 30 minutes). They have been adopted by hundreds and hundreds of local governments throughout the United States.

I served on the Davis City Council for 12 years (three terms of office) from 1984 to 1996. During that time, I served 4 years as Mayor (two terms). During my 12 years on the Council, I never missed a meeting or a vote and was considered kind of the Iron Man of local government. My service on the Council let me to the next step in my local government career. As I was wrapping up my last year on the City Council in 1995, the long-serving and well-respected County Supervisor Betsy Marchand had announced that after some six terms and 24 years of service as a Supervisor she would retire from the Board and would not run again in 1996. Hearing this, I threw my hat in the ring and formed a campaign committee.

The Board of Supervisors has a totally different culture from the City Council, and has a completely different slate of issues. The culture difference is a creature of the times that the two bodies meet. City Councils tend to meet in the evening – so the meetings are heavily attended and City Council members are citizen politicians – effectively part time government officials. Boards of Supervisors meet during the day – so the meetings are sparsely attended by the public and members of the Board are considered employees of the county with staff and offices. In Yolo County, Supervisors receive a salary commensurate with a half-time position. Plus, the issues are generally different. City Councils tend to deal with sewers and zoning and garbage and city street repairs. Boards of Supervisors tend to deal with health and welfare and other human service issues. Of course, issues overlap such as where cities and counties try to divvy up the tax pie, and jointly plan development and land preservation. So, with Betsy retiring I saw an opportunity to delve into a whole new realm, now that my appetite was whetted with local government service.

As the deadline to file for the open position approached, I was both amazed and delighted that no one else had filed to run against me. It looked like I was going to be elected to an open slot with no opposition and no campaign. That was quite different than City Council elections. In the Council election, everyone runs against everyone else and the top vote getters get elected. In the Board of Supervisor election, it's not a free-for-all. Supervisors are elected in districts – five to be exact – and my district was District 4. No one had filed until the last day, and then I discovered that one person had, indeed, filed on that last day to run against me for the District 4 slot. The person who filed was a shocker to me. It was the husband of my campaign treasurer. I barely knew the man. I had met him a couple of times when he popped in to talk to my campaign treasurer or sit through a part of my campaign meeting. In my eyes, this was an amazing local double-cross. Of course, I asked my treasurer to resign, which she did. It was awkward, but had to be done.

The election was fun. Lea and I walked precincts and campaigned hard. I had run many times in the past, had a good reputation and good name ID. It didn't hurt that Betsy Marchand endorsed me and spoke well of me. I raised a lot of money and spent it well. Local county supervisor elections are the one office that has no limit on the amount of money a candidate can raise from a contributor, and after 12 years in local government, I had no problem raising funds to run a strong campaign. District 4 was interesting as it included areas outside the City of Davis – which was new turf for me. Part of the district included the very Republican enclave of El Macero, and another part of the district included a large chunk of the City of Woodland and a heavy Hispanic population. I recall my opponent had no real platform other than he was "not Dave." That didn't carry him very far, and I won handily. He and his wife subsequently moved out of Davis soon thereafter and I never saw either of them again. Nor did I want to. In 1996 I was elected and in January 1997 I was sworn in as the District Four County Supervisor.

To say that I enjoyed being a county supervisor is an understatement. It was a great job. I had an excellent district which included the eastern and southern parts of Davis, El Macero and

Willowbank, the eastern part of Woodland, and a large chunk of unincorporated land between Davis and Woodland. I worked the district during my entire tenure, and spent a fair amount of time with the different components. Neither El Macero nor Willowbank were within the City of Davis, so the Board of Supervisors was, essentially, their city council. There was an El Macero Service District and a Willowbank Service District – each with its own board, and I worked with both of them. The folks there got to know me and supported me over time. As a County Supervisor I served in Woodland, the county seat, but I was also entitled to have a district office, and I set one up in Davis. I wound up serving a total of seven years on the Board of Supervisors, running for a second term in 2000 and being re-elected without opposition. Members of Boards of Supervisors in California have no term limits and tend to serve lengthy terms in office – and I have no doubt that I could have done the same, had I chosen to do so.

My Board colleagues twice elected me to serve as Chairman of the Board of Supervisors. I served as a County Supervisor for seven years, from 1997-2003. As a Supervisor I was entitled to have staff – a Deputy. My first Deputy was Chad Carlock who worked hand-in-hand with me both at the county and in my law practice. My second Deputy was Mariko Yamada – a really sharp, hard-working and savvy young lady. When I left the Board to become a Judge, I spoke to the Governor about Mariko and he appointed her to replace me and fill out my term in office. Mariko went on to win election to a second term on the Board in her own right, and subsequently went on to higher office, being elected (after a difficult campaign against the popular Mayor of West Sacramento) as a member of the California State Assembly. She served in the Assembly with distinction.

Davis actually wound up with two supervisors out of the five because of our population. And the second Supervisor from Davis was Lois Wolk, whom I had served with on the Davis City Council in the 1990's.

My over-arching issue on the Board of Supervisors was protecting farmland from the encroachment of cities. Over my seven years on the Board, I achieved that goal. Yolo County was a recognized leader among California counties in land preservation. We not only protected farmland, we also preserved environmentally sensitive sites. During my time on the Board, I also served as Chair of the Yolo-Solano Air Quality Management District, and as Chair and Board Member of the Yolo Bypass Wildlife Area. I also was energetic in the area of criminal justice, setting up (with Bill LeBov, the Presiding Judge of the Yolo Superior Court) the county's first Criminal Justice Cabinet – bringing together all the leaders in Yolo's criminal justice system – it was co-chaired by the Presiding Judge and me as Chairman of the Board. Years later, in one of life's ironies, I co-chaired it again, but this time as Presiding Judge of the Court.

On September 11, 2001, the United States and the world was shocked when Islamic terrorists hijacked commercial airliners and crashed them into the packed World Trade Center in New York City. Thousands of innocent civilians died and the entire structure was destroyed. In my capacity as a county supervisor, I contacted authorities in New York City and was able to make arrangements to obtain a portion of a steel girder from the WTC. I arranged for it to be shipped to Yolo County and a display was set up in the County Administration Building featuring the steel from the WTC. It was singed and scarred, but was still intact – and remains in Yolo County as a memorial to the lives that were lost, and a reminder of the need for vigilance.

During my time on the County Board, all departments provided the services to residents that our laws and ordinances mandated, the budgets were balanced, and there were no disruptions or scandals. We ran a tight ship. I had a good run as a County Supervisor. I had accumulated a very large nest egg in my political campaign fund (well over $150,000), I had my sights on either running for a third term on Board in 2004, or running for an open seat in the California Assembly. And then, in 2003, my life took yet another sudden turn.

When I served as Mayor of Davis, I would take a page from "Peanuts" and open a table at the Davis Farmers Market to meet with constituents. Here, Lea and Dave staff the table on a Saturday morning in the park.

I debated Rush Limbaugh for one year on television – live, unscripted and unrehearsed. Here we are featured in an ad in TV Guide.

Twenty-Four

The Governor Gray Davis Years

Gray Davis was my immediate boss during my final year-and-a-half with Governor Jerry Brown. Gray was Chief of Staff and I served as Deputy Chief of Staff. We had a good working relationship – not chummy by any means, but professional and respectful. After his time with Jerry Brown, Gray continued in political office. He was elected to the California Assembly, then as California State Controller, and all the way up to Lieutenant Governor. As Lieutenant Governor, Gray had a very small staff, and from time to time he would call on me to help answer some legal or policy questions. I was happy to volunteer my time. I also did my best to help him politically, holding a couple of fundraisers for him and participating in others. Eventually, Gray was elected Governor in 1998, being sworn into office in January 1999.

I was delighted when Gray was finally elected Governor. I must say that the years between the end of Jerry Brown's terms as Governor and the election of Gray Davis as Governor in 1998 were difficult for me and for all Democrats. Those years featured 16 straight years of Republican Governors – two terms by George Deukmejian and two terms by Pete Wilson. Those Republican Governors ran pretty rough-shod over any Democratic office-holder. For example, those Governors tried again and again to evict Gray, the Lieutenant Governor, from the State Capitol Building. It was a long-standing tradition that the Lieutenant Governor's office was located on the first floor of the State Capitol Building, right across the hall from the Governor's Office. That didn't stop the Republican Governor's from trying to extricate Gray from the Capitol Building and move him and his small staff into a state building away from the Capitol. Gray enlisted my legal help to prevent this, and I'm pleased to note that we were successful.

During those Republican-dominated years, Lea and I hosted a number of fundraising events at our home for the Democratic candidates for Governor and had high hopes for their elections. I hosted Los Angeles Mayor Tom Bradley who was the Democratic candidate twice, Kathleen Brown who was State Treasurer and the charismatic sister of Jerry Brown, and Diane Feinstein, Mayor of San Francisco who would later be elected as a Senator from California. They all were defeated by Deukmejian or Wilson.

But Gray won. In 1998 he ran against my old law partner Dan Lungren, and beat him fair and square. Gray wound up with a very strong 58% of the vote to Lungren's 42%. After the long democratic drought, when Gray took the oath of office in January 1999, I was energized. Many of the people he brought into his administration and on his staff I knew from my days with Jerry Brown. One of them was Lynn Schenk, who Gray appointed as his Chief of Staff. Lynn had served in the Jerry Brown administration as Secretary of the Business, Transportation and Housing Agency – a huge agency and a cabinet level position. As Deputy Chief of Staff for Jerry, I used to chair weekly meetings of all senior staff and cabinet secretaries and got to know Lynn very well. Lynn also served in Congress for a term. She was a sharp and savvy woman. Like Gray, she was a centrist and a pragmatist. She was neither a radical nor an ideologue. She was a get-the-job-done kind of staffer. Her style was very much Gray's style, and it was certainly my style.

Another person who I came to know during Gray Davis' time as Lieutenant Governor, his campaigns and his time in office as Governor, was Garry South. Garry was without question the sharpest campaign consultant I had ever met. He managed Gray's successful campaign for Lieutenant Governor (and served as Gray's chief of staff while he was Lieutenant Governor). He also managed Gray's successful campaigns for Governor. Garry was savvy and tough, a take-no-prisoners kind of manager. But he and I got along famously.

I was a happy camper as a County Supervisor in the late 1990's, but in 1999 I started to get that old itch to get back into state government. I felt that I could help Gray but I didn't want to give up the County Supervisor job. So, this posed a dilemma. Lynn was my greatest booster and really pushed to get me on the senior staff. And she came up with the perfect solution.

I was offered a position on the senior staff of Governor Gray Davis as Director of Intergovernmental Relations. My job would be to act as the liaison between the Governor and local government officials (Supervisors, Mayors and Council Members) from throughout California. And both she and Gray insisted that I continue serving as a Yolo County Supervisor – they felt that it would be good to have a working local elected official serve in the liaison capacity. I readily agreed to this "best-of-both-worlds" solution.

So, that's how I came to be working for my second Governor.

I moved into an office in my old "neighborhood" – the Horseshoe – immediately adjacent to the Governor's private office and then started acting as the conduit between local government and the Governor. Fortunately, with Mariko Yamada as my Deputy back in Woodland, she stepped up her game and covered more and more of the responsibilities of County Supervisor. Even so, I never missed a meeting or vote of the Board.

I found myself in the center of the mix in the Governor's Office. Between 2000 and 2003, my responsibilities slowly morphed and increased with multiple titles, tasks and responsibilities. More jobs were offered, and I found that I could never say "no". The first change added Community Relations to my portfolio. So, my title became Director of Intergovernmental and Community Relations. In addition to the local government responsibility, I now had responsibility to be liaison to ethnic and community groups of all kinds, who wanted access to the Governor. Suddenly, I had a staff of six community relations assistants who were stationed in Los Angeles, San Francisco, Fresno, and San Diego. They all reported to me and I did a fair amount of traveling. At other points in time, I had more portfolios given to me. For about a year, I was the Governor's liaison to all the Native American nations in California, and was involved in negotiating tribal casino compacts – a very complex, political, and thorny endeavor. In many ways, this was my most frustrating assignment, as Gray gave me the responsibility, but he never wanted to make decisions on those compacts – and they languished. I believe Gray had an antipathy to gambling and so we never really consummated any tribal compacts. The Tribes, of course, didn't want to blame the Governor – so I suspect that I got a lot of the blame. Gray developed concerns about the California Lottery – frankly, this was an area that was rife for abuse, scandal and problems. So I wound up being named to the State Lottery Commission and soon became the Chairman. And then, for years Gray didn't appoint a Lottery Director, so I wound up running the Lottery, as Chairman of the Board, for about three years. This was a $3 billion per year business, and during my years I'm proud of the fact that we kept it clean – no scandals, no abuses, and no problems. Other assignments included being the Ethics Officer for the Governor's Office, and Chairing the Victim Compensation and Government Claims Board (formerly known as the Board of Control). I'm pleased to say that we had no ethics violations during my tenure and the Compensation Board did its job with no problems or public embarrassment.

Ultimately, I added an even more prestigious title to my list of titles. The Governor appointed me to be Director of Operations in the Governor's Office. My charge cut across all lines and was to make sure things moved smoothly and things got done. Perhaps my most interesting assignment, however, is when the Governor decided he needed another set of eyes on all legislation. In the past, all legislation went through the Legislative Secretary in the Governor's Office, and the Legislative Secretary's five deputies. Governor Davis, a cautious man, wanted more senior eyes to vet legislation. So four of us in the Office – including me – were assigned to review all legislation and be available to brief the Governor at a moment's notice. Since a thousand bills would come to the Governor each year, this meant that I had to review two to three hundred of them. It was a little awkward superseding the legislative unit, but it's what the Governor wanted, so we did it. I remember traveling to connect with the Governor in cars, on planes, or in his Los Angeles office to review bills and make recommendations.

The weirdest assignment – fortunately a short-lived one – occurred when the Governor lost faith in his Legal Affairs Secretary. The Legal Affairs Secretary is the Governor lawyer. The portfolio is important and broad. The Legal Affairs Secretary is a senior staff position and is normally one of the most influential people on the Governor's staff. Well, at one point the Governor just lost confidence in his Legal Affairs Secretary, but instead of reassigning him or asking him to resign, Gray just said nothing to him and worked around him. He asked that all legal matters be sent to me – and I became his de facto Legal Affairs Secretary. Now, this was an incredibly awkward scenario, since the Legal Affairs Secretary was still in place, still in his office, and still in charge of a unit with several deputies. But there I was, actually doing the work. And at the same time, I had to do all my other jobs for the Governor (plus my County Supervisor gig). I will say that the Legal Affairs Secretary, though shunted to the side, worked with me with professionalism. And we got along, getting the job done – me in front, he in the background. Of course, this was an untenable arrangement, and we did eventually set in motion a process for appointing a new Legal Affairs Secretary. I interviewed the candidate – an excellent lawyer with limited political experience – and Gray appointed him. In a gracious move, Gray gave the ousted Legal Affairs Secretary what we call in government a "soft landing". Gray appointed him to a nice (but minor) Department Director position where he could use his skills. So, all's well that ended well in that episode.

In the Governor's Office and in the press, I became somewhat of a minor celebrity when it was discovered that I carried 5 or 6 cell phones at a time – each a different color. As the ethics officer, I wanted to make sure that each phone was dedicated to (and paid for by) a different assignment. For example, I had a cell phone for to conduct my Board of Supervisor's business, a cell phone for the Governor's office, a personal/political cell phone, a cell phone for the Lottery, and so on. There were even photos of me in the newspaper with my array of cell phones.

In my off duty time I helped Gray politically as much as I could, and I was very pleased when he was re-elected to his second term as Governor. The election of 2002 pitted Governor Gray Davis against a very wealthy Republican businessman, William Simon, who had never held political office but was a solid conservative. It was a tough time for Gray because California was in the midst of an electricity/energy crisis. There were rolling brownouts and blackouts which, naturally, were blamed on the Governor. But Gray still won by a healthy margin.

So, in 2003 we started Gray's second term as Governor, and then the electricity/energy crisis heated up and the Republicans launched a recall campaign against Gray. Subsequently, it was determined that this crisis was a façade – it was the result of market manipulation by oil companies and others. However, this did not stop the Republicans from launching a special recall election in 2003 (permitted under California law) against Governor Gray Davis. To me, this seemed terribly unfair as Gray had just run for office in 2002 and been elected in November and sworn into office in January of 2003. Just a few months later, he had to face another election. It was a nasty election, to boot. Regrettably, Gray was recalled – the first California Governor to face that fate – with 55% of the voters supporting the recall. The fact that the Democratic Lieutenant Governor Cruz Bustamante was a candidate in the recall election didn't help. Republican Arnold Schwarzenegger was elected the new Governor with 48% of the vote and Bustamante got 31% while Tom McClintock, a very conservative Republican, garnered 13%. The remaining 130 candidates split up the other 8%.

So, here we were in the weeks after the recall election not knowing what was going to happen. After all, California had not previously recalled a Governor. We didn't even know when the new Governor would be sworn into office. The recall came so suddenly and unexpectedly that most of us working in the Horseshoe had no alternative plans. I, for one, had not given any thought to what I would do after the Gray Davis administration ended. I was enjoying my County Supervisor stint and had some thoughts about running for re-election to the Board of Supervisors for a third term, or running for the State Assembly.

And then I had a conversation with Burt Pines.

Burt had worked as the City Attorney for Los Angeles, a powerful and prestigious office, and Gray had tapped Burt to be his Judicial Appointments Secretary – the man responsible for advising the Governor on his appointments of Judges and Justices. Burt led a pretty solitary life in the Governor's Office. His role was clearly defined, but limited, and it really did not cross paths with any other staffer. He had virtually no interaction with anyone else in the office. Except me. It was a matter of luck (or fate) that Burt's office in the Horseshoe was situated immediately across the internal hall from my office. So, there were times when we would have lunch together. Most of the time I had lunch at my desk, but when I would go out with Burt, we would go across the street to one of the state cafeterias, or to the basement of the State Capitol which also had a cafeteria. The food was never great, but it was quick.

During our lunches, Burt would ask me if I was interested in becoming a Judge. I admit I had given it some thought, but it was not a high priority. I had thought that this might be something to explore toward the end of Gray's second term, after 2006. But here we were, suddenly in a recall election, and it was only 2003.

Even though no California Governor had ever been recalled, the proponents were well financed by the Republican party, and they had qualified the recall, with signatures, for a special election. The recall was real, and the possibility that Gray might be recalled was also real. A recall election is run in two parts. In the first part the public is asked if they wish to recall the Governor. In the second part the public is asked who they wish to elect if the recall vote in the first part is affirmative. Candidates were lining up, but none of them were formidable – until body-builder and movie icon Arnold Schwarzenegger jumped into the race. California had a history of electing actors (Ronald Reagan). To make matters worse, a prominent Democrat – Lieutenant Governor Cruz Bustamante – jumped into the race after Arnold announced. Cruz was running on a weird platform of vote NO on the recall but vote YES

on Cruz. The entire recall was based on a phony, manipulated crisis – the energy crisis of 2002 – but the fact of the manipulation
would not be revealed till much later in time, well after the election. So the recall was real, and it was upon us.

Ultimately, I did apply for a Judicial Appointment. I didn't
go through the normal process of waiting and interviewing and
vetting – after all the Judicial Appointments Secretary had encouraged me to apply, and the Governor knew me.

The recall election fulfilled the Republican party's dream.
Gray Davis was recalled as Governor, and Arnold Schwarzenegger was elected. My most striking memory of this time was how
Gray Davis handled it. The entire episode was politics and manipulation at its worst, and it was unfair and embarrassing for Gray.
Yet Gray handled it with such grace and civility. He remained se-
rene and unperturbed throughout, and was incredibly gracious and
cooperative with Arnold and his team of staffers chomping to get
into the Horseshoe. And so there we were. Since there had never
been a recall of a Governor, no one knew when the new Governor
would take over, nor whether Gray Davis' appointments in the
last few weeks and days would stick or would be rescinded by the
new Governor. Until sworn into office, an outgoing Governor's
appointments can be recalled by the new Governor. There were so
many question marks – particularly for the senior staff and high-
level appointees. No one had really planned for this. Gray had just
been re-elected in 2002 for a four-year term, and here in 2003 we
were leaving office.

I was one of the lucky ones to receive a judicial appointment
in the last days of his administration. I recall being one of five
such appointments – four to the Sacramento Superior Court and
one (me) to the Yolo Superior Court. The Governor signed the
commission appointing me to the Bench on October 3, 2003. Not
knowing if and when the new Governor might call back and re-
scind the 11th hour appointments, I decided that the better part of
valor would be to get sworn into my new judicial office. I knew
from my days working as Deputy Appointments Secretary that
the appointment of a Judge could be rescinded up until the time

the appointee took the oath of office. That being the case, I made arrangements to take the oath of office on October 10, 2003, a Friday.

I contacted a friend of mine, Judge Bill LeBov, who had just retired from the Yolo Superior Court. In fact, it would be Bill's vacant position that I would be filling. There was some irony in all this. When I worked for Jerry Brown, a position had opened on the Yolo Municipal Court. In those days, trial courts were divided between Municipal and Superior Courts – the latter handling the bigger cases. A lawyer with five year's experience could become a Municipal Court Judge, but a lawyer had to have ten year's experience for the Superior Court. At the time, I had been asked if I were interested in this appointment. I had declined as I was very young (my early 30's) and I was just getting into the heart of politics. Turned out that Bill LeBov received that appointment and served in a long and distinguished career. He became a Superior Court Judge when the Municipal Courts and Superior Courts consolidated in the 1990's. It seemed strangely fitting that Bill should swear me in. And so very early in morning on October 30, I went over to Bill's house in South Davis, and with his wife as a witness, Bill gave me the oath of office.

And, voila, I was a Superior Court Judge.

The fact that I carried separate cell phones for different functions was somewhat unique in Sacramento. But I wanted to keep clean ethical lines between different jobs.

Lea and Dave with Governor Gray Davis at the Rosenberg home in Davis.

Twenty-Five

Adjusting to the Life of a Judge

The hardest part about being a Judge, for me, was the adjustment to the new lifestyle. It turned out to be a sea change for me. I had been very active in the community and very active in local and statewide politics. Lea and I would host political fundraisers at our home for local and statewide elections. I was the go-to guy for charity auctions and would function as a volunteer auctioneer 10-20 times each year. But all that was off-limits to a Judge. Judges can't host political fundraisers or serve as auctioneers raising money from the public for charity. In fact, when I became a Judge I (like all other new Judges in the state) received a book on ethics – 90% of which was dedicated to things that a Judge cannot do.

I also had to resign all my offices, of course. As a Judge, I could not serve as a County Supervisor. So, I resigned that office and all the other offices I held by virtue of my county position. My positions on Gray Davis' senior staff all had to end, of course. But I also was required to resign my work on the State Lottery Commission and the Victim Compensation and Government Claims Board. Those Executive Branch offices were incompatible with serving in the Judicial Branch. I was active with a number of Democratic party organizations – those all had to go – a Judge cannot be active in partisan organizations. I even resigned from the Rotary as I felt it would lead me to conflicts as many of the members were leading citizens in the county or local elected officials.

So, the result of all this was a dramatic lifestyle change, It was a culture shock to me. One day I was immersed in activities. And the next day, I was not. In retrospect, it took me a good 12-18 months to adjust to this change in my life from political to judicial. But, fortunately, the rest of "being a Judge" came easy to me.

I think my years of being Mayor, Chairman of the Board of Supervisors and chairing meetings made the transition to Judge easy. Just like my years in journalism were a great prerequisite to being a lawyer, my years chairing meetings seemed to be the perfect encore to being a Judge. Yet again, my life has been a series of stepping stones – all leading me in a certain direction. So, serving as the person on the Bench in the center of the room came easy to me. I could read a room and be aware of what was going on in that room. A Courtroom is, after all, just a big room with lots of activity, plots and subplots. I had to be cognizant of the attorneys, the defendant, bailiff, court reporter, clerk, interpreters, and other players waiting their turn in the action. These are skills I learned in my government positions, most of which entailed chairing meetings. This skill translated well to the work of the Judge. Essentially, a Judge has to do three things. First, the Judge has to be the stage director of the courtroom – making sure all parts are focused and working on the task at hand in an organized and efficient way. Second, the Judge has to be able to make decisions. Making decisions is an essential and ubiquitous part of the job – a part that many attorneys overlook when they seek an appointment as a judicial officer. Every single day as a Judge I make decisions, sometimes a hundred a day, big and small. If a Judge has difficulty making decisions, or agonizes over the decision beforehand and ruminates over it afterwards – then the job of being a Judge has got to be one of the worst jobs on earth. Fortunately, based on my many years in government service, I had no problem making decisions – and I've always had a clear conscience over every decision I ever made as a Judge. Litigants and attorneys don't want to wait days and weeks for that decision. So, in my case, 99 times out of a 100, I will not take a matter "under submission" for a ruling later. I typically rule from the Bench. It's efficient and it's what the attorneys and litigants want. Third, the Judge has to know the law. This may appear daunting, but it is doable. It's daunting because Superior Courts are courts of general jurisdiction. This means that these courts handle all legal matters in the state of California that are within the purview of the judicial branch. That is an incredibly broad scope. The various codes of the State of California encompass several bookshelves worth of statutes. The case law can be found in hundreds of volumes. The jurisdiction of the trial courts in California is broad – covering civil law, criminal law, juvenile law (both dependency and delinquency), family law, probate, small claims, traffic, and special proceedings like habeas corpus. No lawyer can hope to be knowledgeable or proficient in all.

And that was also the case with me. My law practice had focused on civil litigation, primarily pursuing cases against the State of California and its agencies on behalf of people and organizations who had been denied their rights. So, of course, in my first assignments, I was not assigned to the civil department. I received an assignment to the criminal departments, presiding over the specialty drug courts. I also handled a smattering of criminal proceedings like motions to suppress and preliminary hearings. My process of learning was watching experienced Judges for a day or two, and taking good notes. Yes, that actually works. I also had the assistance of the lawyers. In our adversary system, I had the advantage of knowledgeable attorneys briefing the issues. Usually, the right result was pretty obvious.

I remember my first day at the Yolo Superior Court very well. I reported for duty to the Court Executive Officer (the top staff person at the court) who got me oriented to the Courthouse, and got me checked in with Human Resources and the paperwork that comes with a new job. Then I was scheduled to meet with the Presiding Judge (the "PJ" as they are called in the Superior Courts). In California, there are 58 Superior Courts, one for each County in the state. Each Superior Court is pretty autonomous and independent, and each is headed by a PJ, a Judge elected to the position every two years by his/her colleagues. Some Superior Courts are small with the minimum number of two Superior Court Judges. Some, like Los Angeles, are huge with hundreds of Judges. In Yolo, we were considered a small Superior Court with eleven Judges when I joined in 2003.

We had one of the classic courthouses of California located on Court Street and built in the classical architectural style, columns and all, and with the word "CVORTHOVSE" on the front of the building. However, the courthouse had been built a century earlier with accommodations and courtrooms for four Judges – hardly for eleven. So, the Superior Court in Yolo County was scattered in several buildings throughout Downton Woodland, including two temporary trailers that doubled as courtrooms. In custody defendants were walked in chain-gangs, across city streets from holding cells to the main courthouse; and when they came through the courthouse hallways, everyone in the hall (including jurors, witnesses, victims, members of the public, court staff and Judges) had to flatten ourselves against the nearest wall till they passed by. We were the poster child for a new, modern courthouse.

So, back to my first day. An appointment had been set up for me to meet with the PJ to get oriented and to get my assignment. I was very much looking forward to that meeting. I showed up promptly for my appointment, and then I cooled my heels. The PJ kept me waiting for hours. In retrospect, I knew he was busy with a calendar, but at the time I thought it was incredibly rude and short-sighted. I promised myself that if I were ever in the position of PJ, I would treat new Judges with much more courtesy and respect.

In any event, I soon found myself in "training". The training of a new Judge is actually quite rudimentary. Most of the actual training can be described as on-the-job-trial-by-fire training. The door opens, you walk into a courtroom, the bailiff says "All rise" and you start "judging". My start was almost that simple. I did get a week with a mentor Judge (Judge Arvid Johnson) who explained a few things for me, permitted me to watch him in action for a couple of days, and then sat me on the Bench with him while we divided the cases between us. After that, I was informed that I would take over all the drug courts for the Bench, and so I had the chance to observe Judge Doris Shockley who had been doing drug courts for most of her career. In 2003, Yolo Superior Court ran three separate drug courts: (1) Felony Probation Drug Court; (2) Penal Code 1000 Drug Court; and (3) Juvenile Drug Court. These three drug courts, at the time, was a full-time endeavor and assignment for a Judge. The Court had a full-time "Drug Court Coordinator" on staff, reporting to the Judge presiding over drug courts, and we met with the defendants assigned to these courts on an ongoing, regular basis (sometimes as often as once a week) for "reviews". It was the real deal. Progress and success were rewarded, and misconduct or relapses were sanctioned. It was hands-on for the Judge to compliment, cajole, critique or do whatever was needed to break the cycle of drug and alcohol addiction. For me, it was an excellent introduction to the criminal law, and it was especially rewarding as I could help people change their lives.

One technique I used in drug court to great success was to call new participants to the Bench where I would show them some photos on the computer of several addicts who had started on an addiction path to methamphetamine (or cocaine or heroin) and the devastating physical alteration to their faces and bodies as the drugs worked their horror. Mouths missing teeth, hair stringy and patchy, skin sallow and stretched. I remember many a new defendant (particularly the women) who reacted in shock and tears at these photos. It was terrible, but it was effective.

I enjoyed my time in Drug Court. I felt that I was really making a positive difference in people's lives. I handled these drug courts for two and-a-half years, till 2006, and worked with hundreds of defendants – the vast majority of whom were actually helped to alter their life path through these special courts. Even to this day, I run into people who went through the process, see me, and tell me how important drug court was to them.

One such incident occurred in the Jack in the Box in Davis where I had gone to lunch with my grandson. We were sitting at a table when a very large and burly man came into the restaurant. He took a look at me and walked right over to my table. "Are you Judge Rosenberg?" he asked. I nodded and said, "Yes, I am." He reached over and wrapped me in a big bear hug and said, with a smile, "I was in your drug court. You saved my life, Judge." Those were the rewards of drug court.

In 2006 my assignment changed, and I was given a full

calendar in the Criminal Division of the Court. It is the same calendar I have handled for the next fifteen years. Occasionally I will handle a juvenile dependency case or a juvenile delinquency case when a Judge assigned that calendar is disqualified, and on relatively rare times, I will handle a civil or family law case, or a small claims case, or a traffic case. But 99% of my work is in the criminal law. I enjoy it immensely. Even though my background as a lawyer was on the civil side, I took to the criminal law like a fish to water. I found it fast-moving, interesting, and much simpler than the complexities and nuances of civil litigation. Plus, jury trials came fast and furious, and I thoroughly enjoyed presiding over a jury. As of 2020, I had presided over some 230 criminal jury trials – ranging all the way from misdemeanor DUI's to felony murder cases.

In 2019, I added to my criminal court assignment. I was given – as an additional task – our Mental Health Court and our Addiction Intervention Court assignments. Once again, I was placed in a position where I could help people in the criminal justice system who had mental health issues or addiction issues (be it to drugs or alcohol). It was back to the future for me. These specialty assignments take a lot of time – as we spend time with each defendant, one-on-one – but it makes a huge difference. The folks who make it through Mental Health Court and Addiction Intervention Court have life-changing experiences. For the better.

When I worked in local government and state government holding down multiple positions and multiple jobs, I used to say that my dream was to just have "one job". Well, now I was living my dream. I had just one job: the job of Superior Court Judge. And I was loving it. I looked forward every single morning going to work. My commute time was less than 15 minutes and I was typically the first one in the building in the morning. Every day was fun and an adventure for me. Finally, I had just one job.

But that "one job" paradigm was soon to end.

My appointment as a Superior Court Judge was big news in Yolo County. I left my position as a County Supervisor, and my Deputy Mariko Yamada, was appointed by the Governor to replace me on the Board of Supervisors.

Twenty-Six

Welcome to the World of Judicial Politics

When I became a Judge, I left the world of politics behind me. But did I?

Clearly, I had left the world of traditional partisan politics. I had closed the door to the world of fundraising and campaigning. It is verboten to a Judge. Adjusting to be a Judge was relatively easy for me. Adjusting to the politically cloistered world of a Judge was harder – it took me 18 months to fully adjust to that. I had been immersed in partisan politics for some thirty years – so while I physically stepped away from that world, it took some effort to mentally step away. Not to say there were not benefits in leaving that world. Now, I could rightfully say "no" when folks wanted me to sign a petition, or endorse a candidate, or contribute money to a political cause. And Lea found that to be a quiet blessing, as well. It made her life easier.

But, I soon became aware of the world of "judicial politics." It's a world that exists within the Judicial Branch, but is not often recognized, or even acknowledged, outside of the branch. And I found a niche in that rarified world. There are about 1,600 Superior Court Judges in California, plus 106 appellate court justices, and 7 Supreme Court justices; in addition, Superior Court Judges are assisted by about 380 court commissioners and about 30 court referees. These make up the positions of "judicial officers" in California.

The desire to serve and to lead has never left me. And soon after becoming a Judge, I realized that there were three avenues to service and leadership beyond the typical work of a Judge. First, I was aware that each of the 58 Superior Courts in California selected their own Presiding Judge. This was done every two years by an "election" and vote of the Judges. Second, I came to realize that the Judicial Branch was governed by a Judicial Council, chaired by the Chief Justice. The members of the Judicial Council comprise the policy-making arm of the California Court System. The Judicial Council has 21 members, all appointed by the Chief Justice – typically 10 of those members are Superior Court Judges – the rest are Justices, attorneys, and representatives of the California Senate and Assembly. Third, I learned that there was a California Judges Association (CJA), which is the professional association representing California judicial officers. The CJA is governed by an elected Executive Board of 25 members. Learning all this, I aspired to be elected as the PJ of my Court, to be selected as a member of the Judicial Council of California, and to be elected as a member of the Executive Board of the CJA. Pretty high aspirations for a new Superior Court Judge. I wonder if other Superior Court Judges plan their futures in such detail.

But first things first. In 2003 I was a brand new Judge, although I was older than most Judges, having been appointed later in life. I was 57 at the time of my appointment in October and turned 58 soon thereafter on my birthday in November. It is said that the optimum age to become a Judge is 45 (I suspect this is calculated based on 20 years of service and then retirement at maximum retirement pay). It is unusual for Superior Court Judges to be appointed below the age of 40 or above the age of 50. And here I was coming to the Bench at 57. That said, I don't begrudge this "late" appointment one bit. My appointment at 57 enabled me to experience a dynamic and vigorous career in law, government and public service. Further, my appointment at 57 gave me "seasoning". I certainly was no shave-tail, wet-behind-the-ears jurist when I took the Bench. I had walked around the block of life several times. I had developed a considerable maturity and understanding of the human condition. And, I suspect having a Judge with some gray hair may provide some level of comfort and stability to those folks who find themselves enmeshed in the justice system.

The Yolo Presiding Judge at the time of my appointment was Michael Sweet. I've already detailed how he treated me rudely and with arrogance when I first came aboard. His tenure as PJ ended pretty quickly and Judge Steve Mock became the PJ for 2004-05. Steve Mock was the polar opposite of Michael Sweet. Steve was gracious, kind and even-handed – treating everyone with courtesy and respect. So I had two models of PJ – one negative and one positive – both of which assisted me during my later tenure. When I joined the Bench, we had several Judges who had been on the Yolo Court Bench for a long time: Steve Mock, Arvid Johnson, Tom Warriner, Doris Shockley, Donna Petre, Tim Fall and Michael Sweet. Michael Sweet departed Yolo soon thereafter in an unusual move to the Sacramento Superior Court. These sorts of inter-county transfers happen very rarely and have to be approved by the Governor. None of us know, for sure, why that move was approved. But I didn't mind. We had a couple of new Judges in Judge Kathy White and of course, me. So, the Yolo Bench was destined for a major turnover when five Judges were scheduled to retire: Mock, Johnson, Warriner, Shockley and Petre (along with the departure of Sweet). This would be a sea change for Yolo with half the Bench departing in a very short time. Judge Fall had been a Judge since 1995 (first as a Municipal Court Judge and then as a Superior Court Judge) but he had been appointed at an extremely young age – I believe he was only 35 years old when he was appointed to the Municipal Court – and he was not eligible to retire till he turned 65 – accordingly he would have to serve for 30 years until he could retire at maximum retirement benefits in 2025.

And indeed, we got a flurry of judicial appointments following the retirements. Janet Gaard became a Judge after a career in the Attorney General's Office, Steve Basha joined us after serving as the Yolo County Counsel, Paul Richardson was with the Yolo District Attorney's Office and then was appointed a Court Commissioner prior to his judicial appointment, Dave Reed was a private defense counsel and then a Court Referee prior to his judicial appointment, Sam McAdam was an attorney with a large Sacramento-based firm prior to his appointment, and Dan Maguire, like me, served in the Governor's Office on the Senior Staff of Governor Schwarzenegger just prior to his appointment to the

Bench. So, we had a rather eclectic, and certainly rookie group coming on to the Yolo Bench in a very short period of time.

I made a distinct point of mentoring many of these newcomers – in particular Dave Reed, Sam McAdam and Dan Maguire. Not only was it the right thing to do (remembering my experience with Michael Sweet) but also because I knew I would need their help in the future if I were to assume a leadership position as Presiding Judge of the Court. We also had a Court Commissioner – Janene Beronio – who had been serving in that capacity for over a decade. When a judicial vacancy came up, I urged her to run for the office. It was a big leap for her to enter the world of judicial politics, but after some prodding from me, she did it. I promised I would help her and I did. I had a substantial political account as a county supervisor which I was able to transfer over to become my judicial political account. I used a chunk of that money to help Janene, and also freely gave of my time and advice. She had three opponents running against her for the vacancy, but she won it in the primary election (did not need to engage in a runoff) as she got a majority of votes in the primary. It was a great local victory, and Janene was in my corner from that day forward.

After Steve Mock's 2-year term as PJ, I decided to throw my hat into the ring to become PJ of the Yolo Superior Court. I was a relatively new Judge, and the election was contested. But I had the support of the old guard – Mock, Johnson, Warriner, Shockley – and I was elected for a two-year term from 2006-07. The Judges must have liked what I was doing as, in a rather unprecedented move, I was re-elected PJ for a second two-year term, serving from 2008-09. One of the powers of a PJ is to make assignments (be it civil, criminal, juvenile, family, or probate) and I worked hard to ensure that every Judge had an assignment that he or she wanted and enjoyed. I also restructured the criminal calendar – our busiest calendar which took at least half our judicial resources. We had a terrific backlog of trials. I created a system unlike any in California, where the Judges assigned to the criminal division spent one week in trial and the following week in all pretrial matters. This new system, in the first year of implementation, literally doubled the number of jury trials we could complete. In the prior year we were able to do 55 jury trials. Under the new system we did 115. And we erased the backlog.

As the new PJ for our court, I turned my sights on the California Judicial Council. All 58 Superior Court PJs serve on the Trial Court Presiding Judges Advisory Committee – an entity of the Judicial Council. I was an outspoken PJ and I was known to a number of other PJ's (from my years in the Governor's Office) and I managed to get selected as a member of the 15-member Executive Committee of the TCPJAC. One of the things the Executive Committee did was to make recommendations to the Chief Justice every year for the appointment of a Chair of the TCPJAC and one or two Vice Chairs. On the day that the Executive Committee was choosing those nominees, Steve White – who was a classmate of mine from law school and who served with me in the Gray Davis Administration and who was also the PJ of Sacramento – asked me to nominate him for Vice Chair. I agreed but also asked him if he would reciprocate and also nominate me for Vice Chair. Steve agreed. And so we were both nominated. Ultimately, the Executive Committee sent five names to the Chief Justice, including Steve and me.

The Chief Justice Tani Cantil-Sakauye knew both Steve and me to some extent. We were all graduates of King Hall at UC Davis. Steve, however, had chosen a path of criticism of the Judicial Council (primarily its staff arm – the Administrative Office of the Courts or AOC as it was known) while I had taken a more supportive position. Ultimately, the Chief appointed me to be a Vice Chair of the TCPJAC, not Steve. And ultimately, the Chief appointed me to be the incoming Chair of TCPJAC in the subsequent year. Steve took an increasingly adversarial role to the Chief and the Judicial Council and was instrumental in becoming President of an organization of dissident Judges called the Alliance of California Judges ("the Alliance" as it became known). I was even invited to join, but I demurred. The Alliance over the subsequent years raised many critical comments about the Judicial Council, the Chief, the AOC, and primarily a project called "CCMS" to provide a unified case management system to all courts.

When I became Chair of the TCPJAC I started a monthly email newsletter to all PJ's in California which became known in the vernacular as "Rosengrams". Most PJ's also forwarded the Rosengrams to their Judges and Commissioners. These missives turned out to be very popular, as I informed everyone of developments at the state level that affected courts and judicial officers. It was the first time that such a monthly informative memo had been sent to Judges.

Also, as the Chair of the TCPJAC, I automatically was given a seat as a member of the Judicial Council. It was a non-voting member position, but I was fully involved with all reports, and all discussions. My work for that year must have impressed the Chief as she appointed me thereafter to a full three-year term on the Judicial Council as a voting member – one of only 10 Superior Court Judges on the Judicial Council.

Ultimately, I wound up serving on the California Judicial Council from 2012 through 2015. My four years on the Judicial Council were both busy and productive. I served on standing committees of the JC during my entire tenure: Executive and Planning Committee, Rules and Procedures Committee, and Litigation Management Committee. Because of my background, I was asked to be a spokesman for the JC on numerous occasions. At one point I was asked to act as oversight liaison on behalf of the JC on the entire courthouse construction program – a massive undertaking to replace old and worn-out courthouses throughout the state. As an aside, I made sure that the new Yolo Courthouse project remained on schedule and focused, and I was especially proud of the fact that we were one of the first of the new courthouses built in the state. The construction started in 2013 and was completed in 2016 – the new Yolo Courthouse is state of the art in courthouse construction. I think it's the most modern and attractive courthouse in the state. It is five stories high with the addition of an underground story for in-custody criminal defendants and juveniles. The five stories encompass 14 courtrooms, a huge jury assembly room, staff offices, and public counters. There are three separate pathways within the courthouse: one for the public, one for Judges and staff, and one for in-custody defendants and bailiffs. This courthouse will serve the people of Yolo County for the next Century.

When I arrived at the Judicial Council I discovered that – even though the JC had been in existence since the 1920's – they had no rules of parliamentary procedure. Council members looked to me on a regular basis to give guidance when parliamentary procedure questions would inevitably arise. Ultimately, at the suggestion of the Chief Justice, the JC adopted a slightly modified version of my "Rosenberg's Rules of Order" that continue to govern their procedures to this day.

During my four years on the JC, there were three major issues which confronted us: (1) CCMS; (2) the AOC; and (3) the Great Recession. The Alliance was constantly leading the blame game criticizing the Judicial Council and the Chief Justice on CCMS and the AOC, and demanding more autonomy for trial courts.

Several years before I joined the JC (and before Chief Justice Cantil-Sakauye took over as Chair of the JC), a great deal of thought had been given to the need for trial courts to develop "case management systems" so that filings and records could be maintained and used electronically. It was correctly predicted that courts would become paperless over time. There were two paths that could be traveled toward that end. On the one hand, the 58 trial courts could develop their own systems of case management; or alternatively, the state (through the Judicial Council) could develop one system that could be used by all trial courts. The JC opted for the latter approach. Hence, the birth of CCMS. And the criticism started almost at the inception – led primarily by the Alliance which played the issue like a fine violin. The JC was not in the information technology business and it was expensive. It was also taking longer than expected and costs kept going up and up. The Legislature was very critical of the cost. Within my first year on JC the criticism of CCMS had reached a fever pitch. I served on the Council when a motion was made (I may actually have made or seconded that motion) to end the experiment with

CCMS and stop the project. It passed with considerable support. (The irony is that at the very end, there was evidence that CCMS would actually work – but it had obtained such a bad reputation at this point that it was untenable to continue.) So, we halted CCMS and charged the trial courts with obtaining their own systems – at this time, there were several private companies that had developed case management systems, so the trial courts were not thrown to the lions. Since that time, every trial court has adopted a case management system from one of those companies.

The second big issue that confronted us during my tenure on the JC was the "AOC". Prior to Chief Justice Cantil-Sakauye coming on the scene, the JC had built a huge administrative bureaucracy called the Administrative Office of the Courts. The AOC involved itself in numerous activities which directly impacted the 58 trial courts, and over the years had generated a great deal of resentment from trial courts. It was felt that the AOC was too large, too expensive, too intrusive, and too powerful. Again, the parade of criticism of the AOC was led by the Alliance, and they directed their criticism not only to the AOC but to the Chief Justice – which was particularly unfair in my opinion. I and other members of the JC pushed for a complete reform of the administrative function of the Judicial Council. The first thing we did was to eliminate the word "AOC" – we removed it from our lexicon. The new term was "administrative staff of the Judicial Council." We also directed that this new entity – which we pared down considerably to save money – would play a supportive role to the trial courts, not a directive or enforcement role. Third, when the Administrative Director (the staff chief) retired, we went through an extensive and transparent process to replace him. I actually wound up serving on the small committee that interviewed candidates and settled on Martin Hoshino to be the new staff director who was ultimately hired by the Chief and the JC. Martin came from the Governor's administration and was a fresh face to the judiciary. These changes were bold, but they were accepted and appreciated over time by the trial courts.

The third issue that we had to deal with was the economic

turmoil created by the Great Recession in California and through-out the United States. That Great Recession hit in December of 2007 and continue till about June of 2009. There were many eco-nomic causes that brought on this financial event, and there were many impacts. People lost their savings, unemployment spiked, and government tax revenues lagged. During the 18 months of the Great Recession in California, the Judiciary was not spared. Case-loads increased while budgets decreased. Managing the decreased revenue stream was a major undertaking for the Judicial Council during the 18-month run of the Great Recession in California.

I thoroughly enjoyed the dynamic years that I served on the California Judicial Council and was pleased that I had had the opportunity to serve. After my tenure on the JC ended, I did a bit of research and found that I had been only the second Judge from Yolo County to ever have served on the Judicial Council and I was honored for the chance to do so.

But it turns out that my service for the JC did not end with the end of my term on the JC. Following my four years on the JC, the Chief Justice appointed me to serve on a newly-created Advisory Committee to the JC: the Advisory Committee on Audits and Fi-nancial Accountability of the Courts. She appointed me to serve as Chair. This committee is responsible for audits of all 58 trials courts, all six Courts of Appeal, and the Supreme Court of Califor-nia – to ensure that all judicial entities are operating correctly and with best practices. It's a prestigious appointment, cutting across many issues, and I thank her for her confidence and trust.

While the Judicial Council represents the Judicial Branch in California, the California Judges Association (CJA) represents the Judges and judicial officers of California. Early on in my judicial career I aspired to be active in the CJA. And I was. I joined one of the standing committees of CJA – the Legislative Relations Com-mittee, employing my knowledge and skills gathered during my years in State Government. Within a few years, the President of CJA asked me to serve as Chair of this committee and I agreed. Subsequently, and for several years, the Presidents of CJA kept re-appointing me to Chair this committee. Ultimately, I changed the name of the committee to be the Governmental Relations Committee to encompass the relationship of Judges to not only the Legislature, but also the Governor's Office. The committee works closely with CJA's professional lobbyists to protect the interests of California's judiciary.

In 2019 I took the plunge to run to serve on the CJA Executive Board. There are 25 members on this board composed of the President, two Vice Presidents, the Secretary-Treasurer, the Immediate Past President, and 20 members elected from districts throughout California. I was nominated and ultimately elected to serve a three-year term as the representative from my district, District 4, which encompassed nine California Counties: Yolo, Sonoma, Marin, Napa, Solano, Lake, Colusa, Sutter and Yuba. As a member of the Executive Board, I have served as the Board's liaison to the Governmental Relations Committee.

As my first year on the CJA Board of Directors ended, the incoming President of CJA asked me to serve on the Executive Committee of the CJA Board – this is a 10-member committee that operates at the highest levels of CJA and deals with the most sensitive and urgent matters confronting CJA. The incoming President also appointed me to serve as Co-chair of a special Work Group to more effectively interact with the California Legislature and California Governor. In addition, the President appointed me to serve on a second special Work Group – the Communications Work Group. These are critical assignments which I take very seriously.

On May 17, 2021, as I write this autobiography, I was elected as Vice President of the California Judges Association. I accept this as a high honor and privilege. Frankly, I cannot think of a greater recognition of my contributions to the Judicial Branch than to be elected to serve and to lead by my peers in the Judiciary.

In 2012 I received perhaps the greatest honor of my judicial career when CJA chose me – out of California's 2,000 judicial officers – for the Humanitarian of the Year Award. I was very appreciative and honored by this award. Even though I became a Judge, I never lost touch with my community. I have always believed that a Judge should remain involved in his/her community, and should not isolate from that community. Primarily through my involvement with the Davis Odd Fellows Lodge, I have been active in supporting and aiding many aspects of my town of Davis and my county of Yolo. In an interesting twist, in 2013, and every year thereafter till the present, I have been asked to serve as a member of the special committee that selects each year's recipient of the Humanitarian of the Year Award.

Twenty-Seven
100,000 Cases Later

Much to my surprise, when I did the math, I determined that from 2003 to 2020, I had handled over 100,000 cases as a Judge.

The vast majority have been adult criminal cases, primarily felonies. But there is a smattering of other case types thrown in. I have handled a fair number of juvenile dependency cases and also juvenile justice (what used to be called juvenile delinquency) cases – primarily when Judges assigned in those areas have been disqualified. To a much lesser extent I have heard civil, family, traffic and small claims court cases. But if I were to venture a guess, I would say that 97% of the cases I have handled were in the criminal law area. In the first three years of my judicial career I heard a great number of drug court cases. And for two years from 2019-2020, in addition to my regular assignment, I have presided over Addiction Intervention Court (the new drug court) and a brand new venture, Mental Health Court. These latter specialty courts work with persons charged with felonies who have serious drug or alcohol addiction issues, and/or serious mental health conditions. We employ a team to work individually with each person in the specialty court – the team is composed of health professionals, district attorneys, defense attorneys, probation officers and a Judge. It's a remarkable program that actually improves lives. It keeps people out of prison. And the recidivism rate is low. And it has a high success rate.

These specialty courts allow the Judge to perform a unique role – part cheerleader, part parent, part enforcer. I have relished my time in these programs. I have seen men and women at rock bottom – sick, addicted, homeless, friendless and acting out in criminal ways. I have seen these same people transformed into steady, hard-working, tax-paying productive citizens, re-connected with their families and society. Not a bad day's work for a Judge.

But, as noted, the bulk of my cases are criminal cases running the gamut from petty thefts and vandalisms, to serious sex crimes, robberies, assaults, and homicides, including murders. Throughout my judicial career, I have treated each case and each defendant as unique. And at every opportunity, I have tried to talk to the parties and attorneys to see if resolution could be achieved. Some Judges don't believe that this is an appropriate role for judicial officers – they believe that the Judge should just be calling balls and strikes and should leave the parties to find resolutions by themselves. That's not my view. I am very active in trying to help the parties achieve agreements to resolve cases, short of trials. In fact, I would venture to say that I am the most active Judge in Yolo County in this regard. I am often called upon by attorneys and other Judges to try my hand at helping the parties to find resolutions. The first thing I do, of course, is ask the parties to tell me about the case. The very next thing I do is to ask the parties if they have made any offers to each other. Somewhat surprisingly, in many cases no such offers have been made. So, I encourage offers as a starting point to resolution. Once an offer is made, I ask the other party if that is going to work or if they have a counter-proposal. In this way, the dialogue is commenced. I shy away from telling the parties "that's a good offer" or "that's a bad offer". The most I would do is say "that's not an unreasonable offer – what do you think?". And if the parties seem like they have reached a stalemate, I do not hesitate to make suggestions. I don't make "offers" – Judges shouldn't do that. However, I will probe their positions by asking "have you considered this?" Sometimes, when I ask them to consider "this" it opens the door to further discussions.

In the overwhelming number of cases, resolution short of trial is possible, and I try to encourage it early in the process. However, there are a small percentage of cases where resolution may not be in the cards, and these are the cases that wind up going to trial. In my years on the Bench, I have presided over some 240 criminal jury trials. Why do some cases go to trial while most others get resolved through a plea agreement? Several reasons.

First, the parties may be very far apart in their analysis of the case. Second, the defendant may truly believe that he/she is innocent and it is very hard to achieve a plea agreement when the defendant believes he/she did nothing wrong. Third, the offer by the district attorney may be precisely what the defendant would achieve if the defendant went to trial and lost; in that case, there is no real downside going to trial and rolling the dice on the off-chance that the jury might acquit, or that there might be hung-jury which might elicit a new, better offer from the district attorney. In any event, these scenarios result in a very small number of cases that go to jury trial. But while the number of trials may be small, they take up close to half a Judge's time. In other words, I may be in a trial for a full week on just one case; but in the subsequent non-trial week, I may be hearing 250 cases. Do the math. Every trial that is avoided frees up a considerable amount of time for the parties and the Judge to handle other matters.

Most of my cases have been fairly mundane, although obviously important to the parties. But some have been highly interesting and provocative, and have achieved a high-level of public interest. Three such high profile cases come to mind.

First, is the case of the nightclub stabbing that resulted in the death of the victim. There was a Thai Restaurant in the City of Davis called Ket-Mo-Re. It was located right in the Downtown of Davis, at the corner of Third and G Streets. During the day, it was a restaurant and up-scale bar, but after 10 p.m. it transformed into a nightclub, with loud music and a raucous bar scene complete with DJ's and bouncers. On one such night a group of family members with their UC Davis students were in the nightclub celebrating a wedding. One of the participants in that family group was a man from the Los Angeles area who had come to Davis for his sister's wedding. The club was fairly busy and the dance floor was crowded. Another group of young men and women came into the club and started drinking and dancing. The men in this group were members of a gang, or gang wannabes. At one point, with alcohol and women as the fuel, words were exchanged, and a small fight ensued between members of the two groups. The fight escalated until several members of the two groups were engaged. It developed into a melee. One of the gang members was not directly engaged in the fight, but hung back as if he were an observer or lookout. As the fight heated up, the young man from Los Angeles – a very large and husky individual – seemed to be getting the better of the gang members. The fight escalated. And then at one point the gang member who had been hanging back quickly moved into the center, flashed a knife and with one movement plunged the knife into the thigh of the large UCD student, cutting the femoral artery, and then rapidly exited the nightclub. The young man from Los Angeles collapsed and bled to death. He died on the floor of the nightclub that evening. One medical witness at the subsequent proceedings testified that the wound was fatal, and there was no way the student could have been saved by medical personnel that night.

The case went to a Grand Jury which issued indictments against six men, accused of being gang members involved in the crime. The stabber was charged with murder, and his five friends were charged with aiding and abetting. They were all charged with gang enhancements and faced life in prison if convicted on all counts and enhancements. During the subsequent hearings, it was learned that in gang culture one member of the gang, who is armed, typically hangs back in these circumstances and intervenes if there is trouble or a fight – which is precisely what happened in Ket-Mo-Re that evening. In gang culture, the gang can't be seen as weak or losing, so the gang must use such force as is required to "win" every fight. It was also learned that gang members are taught how to wield a knife so that the wound can be very serious or fatal, including the locations in the thigh that would impact a vein or artery.

Ultimately, the defendants entered into a plea agreement. The gang member who stabbed the victim "took the rap" and pled no contest to the charge of voluntary manslaughter, plus a gang enhancement, in exchange for the other gang members having the case dismissed against them. The district attorney conceded that the case of aiding and abetting against the other five defendants was a hard case to prove. With all charges in this case (and another case of assault against another inmate that he picked up while waiting for trial), I ultimately sent the stabber to state prison for close to 30 years.

Second, is the case of the drug-addled mother who took her baby into the swampland around the Yolo County community of Knights Landing, where the baby died after a cold night of exposure. In addition to the tragic death of the baby, and a long prison sentence for the mother, this case prompted significant changes in the way CPS (Child Protective Services) does its job. The mother in this case was under the thrall of a boyfriend who was the ultimate "bad influence." He supplied the mother with drugs, and life between them seemed to be little more than a drug-fueled sexual orgy. The baby was an impediment to the boyfriend's "lifestyle". Because of the mother's drug addiction, the baby, a little boy, was born with drugs in his system – the hospital reported this to CPS, and although the mother was permitted to bring the baby home, CPS was monitoring and implemented a so-called "safety plan" which included other adults in the house. The safety plan did not provide safety to the child.

The boyfriend was not satisfied with sex with one woman, however, and apparently was having an affair with another woman in Knights Landing. One night after a bout of sex with the mother – which included significant use of methamphetamine – the boyfriend left their house in Woodland, and mother, suspicious went to Knights Landing in an apparent effort to locate the boyfriend. Rather than leave the baby behind with relatives, the mother took the baby with her. Her state of mind was clearly affected by drugs – the boyfriend had administered what he called "butt shots" to the mother – that is meth delivered into the body through the anus. But even worse, the boyfriend had convinced the mother that the world was soon coming to an end and that the only safe place would be the swampland of Knights Landing. So in this addled, and slightly hallucinogenic state, mother drove her car to Knights Landing, and with the baby clothed only with a simple onesie, made her way into the thick brush next to the Sacramento River which ran next to that community. In her trial, she said she was looking for the boyfriend. However, she soon became disoriented and weak. She propped the baby in a sitting position next to a tree and fell asleep. How long she slept is unknown. But when she woke up, the baby – still propped up against the tree – had died in the cold and the elements. Mother eventually stumbled out of the swamp, flagged down a local resident and law enforcement arrived. The trial drew great public interest due to the bizarre death of a child. The trial presented a challenge to the jury since the mother's mental acuity had been diminished by the use of drugs. The mother was eventually convicted of second degree murder and is serving a prison sentence of 15 years to life. CPS took steps to reform how it monitors newborn babies who are born with drugs in their system. And the boyfriend didn't escape the fates, either. Although he was not charged in the baby death case, the boyfriend was inevitably going to come in conflict with the law – and he did in other cases – ultimately he was sent to prison for six years. The case presented a plethora of thorny legal issues and was taken up on appeal. In a 37-page ruling, the Court of Appeal upheld my handling of the case, my rulings and the sentence. That he is a different person now.

Third, is the case of the rapist who terrorized both Sacramento County and Yolo County. Turned out the rapist was a former prison guard who hid out in plain sight in Georgia until DNA evidence brought him to justice. He had committed serial rapes in Sacramento, and also kidnapped and raped a jogger in Davis in 1994. The rapist wore a ski mask and viciously abused his victims. He was finally brought to justice in 2020, sentenced in Sacramento and then before me in Yolo County pursuant to plea agreements which netted him 35 years in state prison. It was only through persistent police work that the case was cracked and the perpetrator tracked down. Since he was 60 years of age at the time of sentencing, he may very well live and die in custody.

I took his plea in the Yolo Superior Court to the Yolo case and sentenced him on December 11, 2020. The Davis victim, a very brave and strong young lady, spoke eloquently at the sentencing hearing, as did her mother. The crime that was committed changed the trajectory of their lives and has haunted them for almost three decades. It was apparent to me that being able to present victim impact statements was a cathartic moment for both of them, and so I let them speak for as long as they needed to. During the entirety of their statements, the defendant sat with his head bowed and never looked at them. Both the victim and her mother wanted the defendant to acknowledge the crime and wanted to hear him say he was sorry. The victim was accompanied to court by over a dozen friends and family members who had provided support and comfort to her over the years. At the conclusion of the victim statements, I did something I rarely do – I asked the defendant if he wanted to say anything before I remanded him to serve his 35-year sentence. He thought for a moment and then spoke. In a slow and halting voice, broken at times by emotion, he apologized to both the victim and the mother (and also to the Sacramento victims). He said that he was truly sorry for what he did 27 years earlier, that he is a different person now, and that he had found some measure of solace in God. I believe these words will help the victims in the journey toward healing and peace.

Superior Court Judge Dave Rosenberg in 2020

Twenty-Eight

The Pandemic of 2020

Nothing could prepare us for the arrival of a novel corona-
virus which caused a deadly disease called "Covid-19". It was the
Pandemic of 2020 and it hit the United States – hard – in March of
2020. And everything changed.

On Friday, March 13, I had just completed the process of
choosing a jury for a felony trial and had sent the jury home with
instructions to come back on Monday to start the presentation
of evidence. And then, over that weekend the Governor issued a
stay-at-home order and the Yolo Presiding Judge, on instructions
from the Chief Justice, directed all Judges and employees over 65
to stay at home until further notice. Jurors were told to stay home
until further notice.

Like everyone else, I went to the grocery store and purchased
a number of staples, preparing for the unexpected. For whatever
unknown reason, people all over the world purchased tons of toilet paper and started hoarding it – as if it was a diarrhea epidemic
and not a corona virus. I, of course, bought my share of toilet
paper – but more importantly, I bought staples like flour, beans,
canned tuna, pasta, and other items that I put in what I called my
"Mormon box" much to Lea's amusement. It turned out to be a
bizarre time and also an unexpectedly beneficial time.

On the bizarre side, I became a virtual Judge. The Yolo Superior Court hardly missed a beat. Although I was working from
my home office (rather than in the courthouse) I continued to run
a criminal department using zoom technology. In fact, almost everyone appeared via zoom. Prosecutors, most defense attorneys,
witnesses and defendants – 95% of the time – "appeared" in court
via zoom. And that included me, as the Judge. (Yes, everyone had
to take a crash course in a new technology.) In a weird way, it

was almost better than in person appearances. For one thing, the participants were rarely late, so court ran on time. I also found that I had a better view of witnesses. As a Judge in court I could see witnesses by profile because of the placement of the witness seat next to the Bench. On zoom, I had a full-on unobstructed view of the witness' face. Of course, there were technical challenges. Documents (such as plea agreements) had to be faxed to me, rather than handed to me. And instead of signing documents directly, I had to instruct the clerk to affix my signature stamp. But we overcame all these impediments, and for months we ran a virtual courthouse. I sat in my office with a shirt and tie and my robes and it was the equivalent of being on the Bench. I also had numerous meetings with counsel – by zoom or conference call – to resolve cases. Other Judges referred cases to me as well, and I was rather successful in helping the parties find ways to reach plea agreements. And the parties were motivated to try to find solutions. In March I issued an order authorizing the County Sheriff to reduce the population of the jail – to avoid an outbreak of COVID-19 in those facilities. The jail was built to house over 450 inmates. As a result of my order, and the Sheriff's efforts to cull the people held in custody, we were able to reduce the population to around 200. From a public health standpoint, this was the appropriate thing to do.

That said, the one thing we could not do via zoom was jury trials. Those had to be conducted in person, in the courthouse. By order of the Chief Justice, we were able to delay jury trials. But by July, that delay could no longer be sustained, and we were scheduling our first jury trials since February. These were "time not waived" cases with defendants held in custody. It was a challenge getting citizens to come to court for jury service (the response rate was around 50%) and it would take longer to pick a jury because of the necessity to social distance, even in the courtroom. But we did it.

On the beneficial side, I was able to stay home with Lea for month after month. We had been married for well over 50 years, but this was the first time in our lives that we got to be together for such a sustained period of time. Oh, we were both busy at times. I still had to be in court through zoom, but by and large we were together 24-7. And there were very few distractions. No Odd Fellows events, no Soroptimist events, Lea couldn't spend time at the SPCA Thrift Store (she was on the Board of Directors of the SPCA), and there were certainly no parties with friends. Even eating out at restaurants was seriously curtailed during the pandemic. So, it was an amazing time for us to get to know each other. And we didn't drive each other crazy.

Lea had boxes and boxes, and rooms and rooms of "stuff" scattered throughout the house, the garage and the backyard cottage. Lea is a collector. She does not discriminate. She collects all things. Games, puzzles, kewpie dolls, miniatures cars, plates, bobble-heads, books, dice, cartoon characters, odds-and-ends of all kinds. We have boxes full of this stuff. Rooms full of this stuff. Garage bays full of this stuff. God bless her. Lea not only collects the stuff, but she makes sure that other people get things they are looking for. If someone calls Lea looking for a particular thing – Lea is likely to have it. She is like the welcome wagon, good will, and thrift shop all rolled into one. So, Lea was futzing with all her stuff for months. And I must confess, after all these months, there is hardly a dent in the piles.

I did most of the cooking at home and that was enjoyable for me. I like to cook. And Lea enjoys my cooking. I went shopping once a week. We also got fresh vegetables and fruit at the Davis Farmers Market on Wednesday afternoons and Saturday mornings. Other than that, we hardly left the house. We ate out infrequently, and if we did get food from a restaurant it was typically take-out. Most restaurants had to close during the pandemic, although for a time outdoor seating was permitted.

When I wasn't in court, I was writing on the computer. This autobiography was a project I started and finished during the pandemic. I tried to write a bit every day, and succeeded doing so on most days. In addition, I composed the trivia questions that I sent out to hundreds of people every morning, before 6 a.m. I enjoyed coming up with the questions and answers, and I think the daily trivia gave my friends and colleagues a little something to look forward to each and every morning. Outside of that, my only engagements were as a member of the Board of Directors of the California Judges Association, and in my various capacities for the Odd Fellows. It wasn't much – but it was enough.

We wore masks whenever we left the house, unless we were exercising outside. I took a daily walk early in the morning when it was cool. For the first few months, Lea went to two exercise classes every week, also in the morning. We rarely connected with our friends. Perhaps once a month a few of us would gather in the private park in front of our house – socially distanced – to just meet and chat. On occasion I would meet with a few friends in someone's backyard to smoke a cigar and chat some more. But on balance, our lives were very different. It was 95% Lea and Dave, and only 5% with others.

On New Year's Eve we even had a New Year's "party" with a dozen friends. Of course, the party was all on zoom. But it was better than nothing.

When the pandemic started in March, I sent out an email to the 300+ Davis Odd Fellows with 10 trivia questions, and promised to send out another one the next day with the answers to the first day's questions. It replicated our "club nights" that we held at the Lodge where we would play trivia while we had dinner. Well, on Day 2 I sent out the next set of 10 questions. And then on Day 3 did it again. And so on. In March, we had no real idea how long this pandemic, sheltering-in-place would last. We thought maybe a month or two and then we could get back to normal. Well, here we are in April 2021 and I just sent my 400th trivia game, (That, by the way, is 4,000 trivia questions. A LOT of questions. But, again, writing the trivia questions gave me one more thing to do to fill up my time.)

We thought we could get back to normal in May. Then June. Then perhaps at the end of summer. Then we thought the beginning of September. October? November? December? Now we all think that "normal" will never return until a safe, effective vaccine is developed and made available to the world.

And then in November and December the world experienced a "relapse". The virus came back with a vengeance in a second and third wave. Stay-at-home orders were issued. Restaurants had to close even outdoor dining, although take out was permitted.

At long last vaccines were developed and were made available to the public. Lea and I both receive the Pfizer vaccine – a first dose and a second dose. We now feel more protected against the deadly virus, and normality is slowly returning to California. We even have plans to visit our daughter and her boyfriend in Texas in June, and our son, his wife and our grandson in New York at the end of August. But we recognize that the virus is a tough enemy, and when rates go down in one locale, they rise in another. I suspect the virus – and its mutations – will be a reality for the human race for many years to come.

So, we live in the world of the pandemic. And we appreciate each other. We value the small things in life. We value life.

*During the pandemic I took a long walk every morning –
obviously masked and social distanced.*

I had a "Zoltar" built in 2015 and donated it to the Davis Odd Fellows Lodge. Zoltar sits in the lobby to welcome visitors. During the Covid-19 pandemic, I put a face mask on Zoltar to display the proper etiquette of mask wearing. He was a good role model.

*During the pandemic, I never missed a day of court work,
although I had to do it from my home office, on zoom.
What a strange way to run a courtroom. But I did it!*

Twenty-Nine

My Family

Unquestionably, I have dedicated my life to public service – this started when I joined ROTC at the age of 17 in college – knowing that it would lead to a 6-year commitment as an officer in the US Army upon graduation. And that public service has continued to this day as I enter my seventh decade of life. In fact, public service has been the focus of my life throughout the years of my life. I love to work and I love to help others. So much so, that "retirement" to me is a bit of a dirty word.

Inevitably, this focus on public service has impacted my family life, and I regret that. Perhaps that is the single greatest regret of my life. But, in spite of my focus on work and community service, things turned out relatively well for my family.

Any discussion of family must start with my wife, Lea. In 2018, Lea and I hit that magic number of 50. On June 30, 2018, we celebrated our 50th wedding anniversary. We are now well past 50 and going strong. A little-known fact is that less than 5% of American marriages last 50 years. So we are in a very small, elite and select group. In our 20's and 30's we wonder what is considered "old". Is it when you hit 40? Or 50? Or 65? Well, I can tell you that when you hit 50 as a wedding anniversary, one thing is certain: You are old. You are certainly going to be in your 70's, at least. But just because one is old, doesn't mean one is ready for a rocking chair on the front porch. Lea and I are both active in the home and in the community.

Just like someone who turns 100 years of age, folks who hit 50 years of marriage (to the same person) are inevitably asked: "What's the secret?" As I reflect on my marriage, and many other married couples I have known, I must say that there is not one answer that fits all couples. A lot depends on the personalities of the two people. I can say that in the case of Lea and me, our married longevity is primarily based on tolerance. I can be a very "take-charge" kind of guy. A little "Dave" can go a long way. Had I married a "take-charge" kind of gal, we would have been at each other's throats. Lea has a much more mellow and laid back personality. So we fit each other like a hand in a glove. I have always tried to do what I can to make sure that Lea is happy and content. So, it's the little things that matter. I know Lea likes to go shopping for shoes and clothes – so I take her shopping for shoes and clothes. I know Lea likes to collect things – so I tolerate her hundreds of collections. I like to cook so Lea lets me do the cooking.

Admittedly, I have a very small family as my relatives were generally murdered by the Nazis in World War II. Only my parents and one uncle (my mother's brother) survived the Holocaust. I've already talked about my parents – Harry and Fay – in an earlier chapter. Apparently, I was the apple of their eye as they followed me into my adult life. When I moved to California, they ultimately followed. When I was in college on the Central Coast they settled within 200 miles from me in Los Angeles. When I moved to Davis, they moved to Napa to be near to me – Napa is only an hour's drive from Davis. When my father passed away, I helped my mother to sell her home and moved her to Davis where she lived till her death. My uncle, Joe, had no connection to me ever since my father and he had a falling out. I have not seen nor heard from Joe, nor his family members since the 1950's. My father and mother were clearly affected by the Holocaust. My father, however, never ever talked about it. My mother rarely talked about her experiences in the camps – but (when I pressed her) she did share some stories of misery, fear, cruelty and death that no one should ever have to experience, let alone a young girl.

I have a younger brother, Mitchell Lonnie Rosenberg. He was born in 1960 and so I am 14 years his senior. I usually feel more like an uncle to him, rather than a brother. I had a very brief relationship with Mitch because I left home in 1964 to attend college. I was 17 and Mitch was not quite 4. I suspect my leaving was a bit of a shock to him. One day I just left to go to the airport, and didn't come back. Mitchell's adult life hasn't been an easy one. He worked for awhile – had a good well-paying job – and then suffered some mental health breakdowns. He has been dealing with failing health and mental health issues for years. He lives in California, primarily supported by social security and county in-home supportive services, and I try to help him from time to time.

I am quite proud of my two children.

My son, Jason Harris Rosenberg, was born in 1971. His early years couldn't have been easy because that was the year I started law school. So for the first three years of his life, I was a law student – a very consuming endeavor. And then immediately after graduation, I started commuting to and from Sacramento in various positions working for a Federal Judge, two Governors and law firms. Plus, there was always the second layer of my life – my political involvements and my service in local elected positions. Notwithstanding all these distractions, I tried my best to be a good, steady father to my son. We took family trips together, and I sent him to a wonderful summer camp for a couple of summers – called Kennolyn in the Soquel Mountains (near Santa Cruz). Lea had attended this very camp as a child. I think Jason enjoyed it in his own way. Although there is a family legend that one summer we forgot to attend family day and he had to tag along with another family that day. I don't think that's true, but Jason sort of believes it, laughs about it, and I have not disabused him of that notion.

Jason was very much into music and "zines" that he created. He organized and played in several bands including one group he called "Necromancy". He wrote and performed music.

He attended local Davis schools – elementary, junior high school and high school. They are considered some of the best in the State. But Jason never really felt that he fit in those public schools, and he wanted to attend a private school. Although I think Lea and I were pretty liberal in our upbringing, Jason didn't like a lot of rules – and craved more independence. Ultimately, Jason convinced Lea and me and we signed him up to attend a well-respected private high school in Walnut Creek called Athenian. This was a live-in school so he lived in the dorms. Jason seemed to enjoy it and thrive in this environment, and we visited him every couple of weeks. Interestingly, in his final year of high school, Jason decided he wanted to come back to Davis and graduate from Davis High School. And he did.

Jason always did things his way. After high school he continued with his bands and they went on tour throughout the United States and Europe. He had some success with his music, and to this day receives small stipends from ASCAP.

Ultimately, the music gave way to employment in the design industry, and he developed amazing skills and quite a reputation. What is remarkable to me is that Jason had a sixth sense for design, and always seemed to be a step ahead of the general public. He did not have a college degree but his street savvy was what his employers wanted. And he has worked form some major companies and clients – Gap, Pepsi, Johnson and Johnson – designing their product look, packaging, displays and marketing. He worked in San Francisco for a while and then ultimately moved to New York City – that's where the action was in the field of design. Jason worked for several major companies and also design studios and is highly regarded in his field. Jason married a wonderful young lady by the name of Carmen Ruiz-Davila (part Cuban and part Puerto Rican), bought a house in Brooklyn, and had a child whom they named Julian. This little boy is sharp as a tack, highly active, and seems to have remarkable soccer skills – plus he is left-footed which is much in demand in the soccer world. We may hear more from him as an adult in soccer. Carmen and Jason have enrolled Julian in the International School of Brooklyn, where he is taught in both English and Spanish.

My daughter, Janis Ellen Rosenberg, was born in 1977. At that time I had just started working on the senior staff of Governor Jerry Brown so I was gone quite a bit and was always "on call" to the Governor's Office. At home, as Janis grew older, she and Jason would nitpick at each other like most siblings – driving each other and their parents a little crazy. Janis attended the Davis school system for elementary school and also junior high school and was in every respect a normal and well-adjusted kid. Then, something happened in junior high school that affected her in some way – although I never really found out what it was as she was not forthcoming. But she did not want to return to the junior high school and Lea and I respected her wishes. So we signed her up for a private school in Sacramento, called Country Day School. Janis seemed relatively happy there. She also attended the Kennolyn Summer Camp and seemed to enjoy that quite a bit – and can sing the Kennolyn Camp song to this day.

Janis became a bit of a wild child for a period of time. I won't go into all the details of this wild period of Janis' life, but suffice it to say that it got to the point where I told her to leave the house. And she left with her boyfriend at the time, Jeff Jorgensen. I didn't have much contact with her for quite a while, and then learned that she was pregnant, with her boyfriend. Janis had a difficult pregnancy. In 1997, Janis gave birth to my grandson, Jonathon Guy Jorgensen. Janis and Jeff ultimately did not get along and drifted apart. Jonathon grew up a sturdy little boy, sometimes living with Janis and sometimes living with Lea and me. At one point, Janis met a decent young man by the name of Christopher Samms and they got married. That marriage, after some years, ended in divorce, but Janis and Christopher left as friends.

Jonathon also went to Kennolyn Camp – so a third generation camper, and I think that provided him some of his happiest memories. Jon graduated from high school and had a wonderful high school trip to Greece which provided him amazing memories. Jon took some college courses, but as many young men do, is still finding his way.

Janis is a very talented young woman. She had a good business head on her shoulders, had great fashion sense, and was amazingly talented in design. One day, I asked Janis what her dream was and she told me that her dream was to own a ladies clothing boutique. I told Janis that I would help her realize her dream. And so, Janis launched a boutique which she named "Shorty PQ's". She was living in West Sacramento at the time, and the shop was located in a shopping center just a couple of blocks from her house. After a couple of years, she moved the boutique – lock, stock and barrel – to Old Town Sacramento. I must say that Janis did an incredible good job running the boutique. She designed everything from the advertising to the bags, to the clothing tags, to the layout. The fashions she chose for the boutique were top-notch. She had employees and displayed excellent management skills. I was very proud of her. Nevertheless, after a few years, the business had to close as it was just not profitable – which I attribute primarily to location. She gave it the old college try.

Ultimately, Janis decided to take a leap of faith and move to Texas. She had a friend or two in that state and had visited it once or twice, but in actuality she knew no one. She decided to move to Conroe, Texas, several miles north of Houston. I asked her once why she wanted to make that move, and she told me that she was looking for that special someone: "Dad, everyone in Davis is either too young, too old, or married." So, I helped her move by selling her home in Davis and using the money to purchase a home in Conroe which I had her take in her name. After a few months in Texas, Janis called me and said: "Dad, I've made the biggest mistake of my life. I'm really unhappy here and want to come back to California." That was distressing news to me, but I told her to sleep on it, wait a few days and then we would see. Interestingly, within a couple of days, everything changed for Janis. She met Chris Stamm – who turned out to be the light of her life. And – like most people meet in Texas – she met him in a bar (actually a bar, restaurant and nightclub) in downtown Conroe where everyone hangs out. I've met Chris several times, and like him a lot. He is smart, personable, and focused. Chris is a relatively young man – approaching 50 – but he is essentially retired, having made a considerable amount of money as a general manager for a large automobile dealership. He invested that money well. Chris and Janis really love each other, and I hope they will wed someday. They are a good match.

My son, Jason, and my daughter, Janis, now check in with me a lot and often seek my advice. So I guess I did reasonably well as a parent. I recently rifled through some old papers and discovered a speech that Janis had given to a group that was honoring me. I found it very revealing to view myself from the eyes of one of my children. In that speech, Janis said:

"Growing up I knew my dad had a very important job. I just had no idea what it was exactly. It didn't matter where we were going, people would stop us and they would introduce themselves and shake his hand. Sometimes, they would carry on, and on in conversation and then part ways leaving with a huge smile on their face. My dad would squeeze my arm and say to me, 'I have no idea who that was.'"

"When I was old enough to drive, I would meet him at his law office in Sacramento for father daughter lunch and shopping dates. His office walls were lined with awards and pictures. I was not quite sure what each was for or who the people in the pictures were, but I did know he was proud of them. After lunch, we would walk to Macy's where he would patiently follow behind me and carry anything I was going to try on. When I was done, we would go to the register to pay and, just to embarrass me, he would try to pay with his Safeway Select card. He still does this, and yes, sometime, it still embarrasses me."

"While dad lived to embarrass me every chance he got, there was a serious side that meant business, too. I learned the five freedoms (speech, religion, press, assembly, and petition for redress of grievances) guaranteed by the First Amendment of the Constitution when he overheard me tell a friend to 'shut up.' The lecture I got about how rude it was, and who did I think I was to silence another person's opinion and thoughts left quite an impression. I have not used the term since."

So, that's my little family. I find myself as the Patriarch of this little clan, and as I am in my 70's that seems appropriate.

Ever since our marriage in 1968, Lea and I would send out a holiday card with a family photo. This family photo stems from 1989, with Jason and Janis. Ah, the teenage years.

Lea Rosenberg has received numerous community honors for her work in Davis. She has been chosen as Citizen of the Year, and also has been chosen multiple times as the "most dedicated volunteer" in the community. I'm very proud of Lea.

My grandson, Julian, is an excellent soccer player.
As a left-footer, he is much in demand.

*The well-dressed men. Here is a photo of me with my
Grandson Jonathan, taken when he was very young.
Jon is in his 20's now.*

My son, Jason, was quite the soccer player when he was young. Now his son, Julian, excels in soccer.

My daughter, Janis, was really into horses when she was young. In fact, there was time she owned two horses, and did a lot of riding. And now she lives in Texas.

My daughter, Janis, and her long-time boyfriend, Chris Stamm, a true gentleman. They live in Texas in the small town of Conroe, and are very happy together.

I've always liked this photo of Lea. Yes, she does love crab.

A photo of my eldest grandson, Jonathon, taken just a few years ago. Jon does love Japanese food.

The "New York Branch" of the family. My son Jason and his lovely wife, Carmen.

Lea with grandson, Jonathon, and "friend".

Thirty

The Independent Order of Odd Fellows

In March of 2004 both Lea and I joined the Independent Order of Odd Fellows (IOOF), specifically the Davis Odd Fellows Lodge. Little did I know at the time that Odd Fellows would become a major part of my life, and a significant aspect of my public service. I was prepared to be Judge, not a Monk.

Prior to March of 2004 I imagine I had no greater knowledge of the IOOF than any other non-Odd Fellow. I do remember walking past the Odd Fellows Lodge in downtown Davis and peering inside through the locked glass front doors. There wasn't much to see, frankly. No lights were on. I could discern a couple of old signs with days and times for meetings. I could make out a black board with removal letters – some of which were missing – identifying the names of some people to contact in case of an emergency. And there was a railing going up to the second floor with one of those old-fashioned single seat chair lifts. There was a sign on the door advertising a local church which held services on Sunday. A stranger to town might have believed that this building was actually a church.

In 2004 I was a little more knowledgeable than the stranger to town. I had, of course, served on the Davis City Council for twelve years, four of which were as Mayor, and I had served on the County Board of Supervisors for seven years. I knew something about Davis and I knew that this building was the Odd Fellows Lodge Hall. But at that point, my knowledge of Odd Fellows ended.

My life had changed in October of 2003 when the Governor appointed me to the Yolo Bench. Once I became a Judge, I resigned from the Board of Supervisors and from all my executive Branch commitments. I was prepared to dedicate myself to the judicial life that had been given to me. But I was certainly not ready to give up my involvement in my community. I needed a private outlet for my energy and desire to continue community service.

It was my good fortune that a long-time friend of mine, Ted Puntillo, whom I had helped become the Veteran's Services Officer for Yolo County (after his retirement as Postmaster for the City of Davis) was a member of the Davis Odd Fellows. In early 2004 when I was looking for a way to stay involved in my community, Ted asked me, almost off-handedly, if I would be interested in joining the Davis Odd Fellows Lodge. Perhaps to his surprise, and somewhat to mine, I said that I was interested. In fact, both Lea and I were interested.

Well, like most Odd Fellows Lodges that get a new prospect, we were rushed into the process and the initiation. Before I knew it, in a matter of weeks, Lea and I were initiated in March of 2004. It's interesting to note that at the time of our initiation, the Davis Lodge had about 40 members on the books – and that, of course, meant that the Lodge had about 20 "active members". Typically, only 10-15 were showing up for meetings. And then a strange series of events occurred.

First, virtually everyone who had come to the Lodge to conduct the initiation disappeared within the next few months – resigned, moved away, or just dropped out. I never saw those people again. Second, the man who was Noble Grand (that's the equivalent of President) of the Lodge when I was initiated got a job in another city and within a very short time he moved away and we never heard from him again. So, in the latter part of 2004, we were a very small group of members – just a handful who had joined in 2004 and a handful who had joined before 2004. During the nominations and elections for new officers that year, I nominated a young man for Noble Grand who had joined about the same time as I did, and he in turn nominated me for the position of Vice Grand (Vice President) of the Lodge. We both won. We were both rookies so we plodded along for a while as best we could, and then the third event occurred. The young man who had just been elected Noble Grand resigned. And so, in 2005 I became Acting Noble Grand, and then Noble Grand of the Davis Odd Fellows Lodge – perhaps the greenest and most ignorant Noble Grand in the history of the Davis Lodge, which had been originally chartered in 1870.

But because I was so green and so new and came into this with no pre-existing assumptions, I was able to discern that for all its great and lengthy history, ritual and strength, Odd Fellows was a dying Order in North America and in California. I started coming to this realization in 2006, and became more fully aware of the problem in 2007 and 2008. Odd Fellows became my hobby and avocation, and frankly, my project. I didn't play golf – instead, I immersed myself in the Lodge and in Odd Fellowship. I was determined to reverse the tide of decline of this old fraternity, and show that it was still relevant and that it could grow. I used my own Davis Lodge as the "laboratory" to show how this could be done. So, three things flowed from this effort.

First, I wound up serving as Noble Grand for four years. This is quite the exception in Odd Fellowship – and it is not a recommended practice. Normally, a new Noble Grand takes over every year. But I needed more time to change the culture of the Davis Lodge. I was determined to show that with some change – the Davis Lodge could grow and thrive; and this could be a model for other Lodges and the Order. So, my starting point was about 30 members. I made some major changes. It wasn't that hard, to be frank, because most of the old timers who would resist change had departed, and we had mostly new members who were enthusiastic about change. And I was a former Mayor of Davis and former County Supervisor (and present Judge) so I had some gravitas and credentials. Members trusted me, and I would not let them down. I polled the membership to determine what they wanted to do going forward. Up to this time, the Lodge was hardly involved in the community and was almost invisible in Davis. I took the polling information and picked the top three items, forming committees to implement. Subsequently, I instituted a committee system to focus our attention on community service and social activities for the members. I created a membership committee (which I chaired and continue to chair to this day) encouraging membership recruitment, particularly of women and ethnic groups who had not been previously represented in our membership. We opened our Lodge Hall to the community, offering many community functions (like music venues), and we made it much easier for members of the public to rent the Lodge Hall for their events. I made sure that we installed neon signs on the Hall so that it was clear we were a Lodge of Odd Fellows. I oversaw a complete remodel of the inside of our Hall – with new carpeting, wood paneling, installation of a stage, and a real elevator. Lea and I initiated or encouraged a plethora of events over the years that exist to this day: Odd Fellows Bingo, Taste of Davis, Breakfast with Santa, the Davis Classic Film Festival, Breakfast with the Bunny, the Davis Chocolate Festival, Thursday Live! Music at the Lodge, the Zombie Bike Ride at Halloween, and many more. These events have become synonymous with the Odd Fellows. At the end of 2020, the Davis Odd Fellows Lodge has 312 members (quite a leap from 30) and 10 applicants for membership (which we call "Pledges" in our Lodge). The Davis Odd Fellows Lodge has shown a net gain in membership every single year from 2005 till 2020 – a remarkable achievement. We are the largest Odd Fellows Lodge – by far – in California, and I believe the entire United States and the world. We have today over 50 Lodge Committees all dedicated to serving the Lodge members or the community.

Second, I decided to get active and involved at the state level of Odd Fellowship. That was neither easy nor simple because no present members from the Davis Lodge had really been involved at the state level. In 2010 I started attending Grand Lodge Sessions which was the once-a-year gathering of all Lodges representatives; the sessions last for four-five days of meetings and ceremonies. I started getting to know the players and getting active at Grand Lodge. One year, the incoming Grand Master Rick Boyles asked me to be one of his appointed Grand Lodge Officers. Specifically, he asked me to serve as his Grand Marshal, which is the most prominent of the appointed officers. I accepted, but

I also decided to run for Grand Warden. The position of Grand Warden is #3 in the hierarchy of Grand Lodge. The Grand Warden is elected by the representatives and serves one year in that position, and then as a matter of routine is elected to be Deputy Grand Master – serving for one year – and then Grand Master – serving for another year. All three of those elected officers also serve on the Grand Lodge Board of Directors, which along with some elected Directors, runs the Grand Lodge operation when not in sessions. Well, turns out I was elected Grand Warden in 2013, so Rick had to find someone else to serve as his Grand Marshal. Subsequently, I was elected Deputy Grand Master and then Grand Master – a position in which I served in 2015-16. I served on the Grand Lodge Board of Directors for seven years, including two years as Chairman of the Grand Lodge Board of Directors. After a one-year hiatus from the Grand Lodge Board of Directors, I was re-elected on May 16, 2021, to a three-year term on that Board.

One of my major contributions as Grand Master was highlighting the need to increase membership, and I was very pleased to see our membership numbers (after decades of decline) start to go up during my tenure. I also shocked the organization when I appointed a majority of women to serve as my Grand Lodge Officers – historically, only two women had ever served as Grand Lodge Officers before my term; during my term four of the seven officers were women. I also moved up in the Grand Encampment, achieving the highest office of Grand Patriarch – one of only 5 or 6 Odd Fellows in the history of California who served as both Grand Master and Grand Patriarch. I was even active in the Patriarchs Militant, achieving the rank of Brigadier General and Deputy Department Commander for California. I even served a term as Judge Advocate General of the Military Department of Patriarchs Militant.

Third, I formed an organization within Odd Fellowship to encourage modernization and change, dubbing it "Dedicated Members for Change" (DMC). In the Fall of 2010 I had some discussions with Don Smith and Rick Boyles about forming this entity and in December of 2010 we created and launched it. Don Smith, who has since passed away, was a legendary Odd Fellow. He served as both Grand Master of California and as Sovereign Grand Master – one of the few California Odd Fellows to achieve that station. He was instrumental in the progress of the Odd Fellows Homes of California – two first-class retirement communities in Napa and Saratoga owned by the Order. I met Don through the retirement homes as we both served on the Board of Directors, and I wound up serving two terms as Chairman of the Board of Directors. Don was elderly but he was far-sighted and progressive. Rick Boyles and I served together in numerous capacities and we both served as Grand Masters of California. Rick is very insightful. All three of us realized that Odd Fellowship was heading toward extinction with the numbers of our members and Lodges sinking fast. In fact, for over 50 years, the numbers had been dropping steadily. So, in recognition that if we continued operating as a fraternity the same way we did for the last 50 years, the results would be the same: decline in members and Lodges. The three of us gathered another 20 progressive Odd Fellows together, and with the help of the Internet we created Dedicated Members for Change or "DMC" as it became to be known. This loose-knit group of like-minded Odd Fellows grew to hundreds throughout California and North America, with even a few members in Europe. At first, we were shunned and marginalized. The "powers-that-be" at Grand Lodge would not even let us have a simple meeting at the hotel during Grand Lodge Sessions. I remember our first meeting during sessions had to take place at a Mexican restaurant three blocks from the hotel. But we persevered. The irony is that we now have a regular event at sessions on Thursday evening, and it is attended by everyone – Thursday is now DMC's night at Sessions. I've also sent out a weekly "DMC Newsletter" for the last 10 years. During that time, I have sent out over 500 such newsletters. Ninety percent of the articles are written by me, but Rick Boyles and Peter Sellars (another Past Grand Master and a writer of some excellent historical books about IOOF) have written several cogent articles. Over those years, I have taken many of my articles and compiled them into three separate books which have been published under the title: The Future of Odd Fellowship. There have been hundreds of books written about the Odd Fellows, all of which focus on the past. I believe my three books are the only ones that have ever been written about the future of the fraternal order. The books have been in great demand and I have mailed copies all over the USA and Canada on request. The focus of the DMC Newsletters, and the three books, is all about what Odd Fellowship needs to do to grow and thrive. Frankly, I used the experiment that I launched at the Davis Lodge to show that Lodges can grow. I have incorporated most of the techniques which have proven so successful in Davis and urged Lodges to consider how they might apply to their experience in their cities. I know several Lodges that have done so to great success and great growth. When Lodges focus on helping their communities and planning fun social events for members, it makes a difference.

So, my little "avocation" in Odd Fellowship has proven, for me, to be an enjoyable, entertaining and challenging endeavor. I have achieved the highest recognition and honors the fraternity can bestow. And I have tried to give back in equal measure. My "experiment" at the Davis Lodge has been an enormous success – bringing that Lodge from 30 members to over 300 – and I believe that success provides a model for the future of Odd Fellowship into the 21st Century.

The Davis Odd Fellows Lodge has become a big part of the life of Lea and Dave. Here, we are participating in the annual "Davis Chocolate Festival", another one of my ideas that proved very successful and popular in the community.

Davis Odd Fellows lined up for the "World's Greatest Bicycle Parade." The Lodge set a Guinness World Record for most bicycles in a single line. Dave is in the very back of the photo.

Thirty-One

The Evolution of My Belief

Most people don't get to choose their belief system or their religion. Generally, this is established at birth. If you are born to Catholic parents, you are considered a Catholic. If born to Protestant parents, you are a Protestant. If born to a Jewish family, you are a Jew. And the same is true of Muslims, Buddhists, Hindus, and dozens of other faiths, religions and beliefs. You are ultimately the child of your parents, and you assume their religion.

For the first five decades of my life, I never really gave this truism much, if any, thought. Frankly, I was not a religious man. I knew my heritage was Jewish (which is both a religion and a culture), but not much else. My parents – Holocaust survivors – never really discussed Judaism, never took me to Synagogue, and never gave me a religious upbringing or education. I suspect that they had their faith drained from their psyche as a result of the horrors they had experienced. In any event, religion was not in the top ten of my issues.

However, that is not to say that I didn't think about the subjects of life, death, truth, honor, love, charity, and all the other aspects of humanity that separate us from the beasts. And that is not to say that I didn't think about God and the concept of God. I believe that I have lived a moral life – a life of honor. I ask myself, why? What is it that directs me to do honorable things, to tell the truth, to not hurt others, to try to live life righteously?

In my 50's I came to realize that I believe in God.

This was, to me, a very significant thing. Faith is not a good subject for debate. You can't "prove" faith like you can prove gravity, or heat or light or mathematics. Faith, ultimately, is a belief, a feeling, that is beyond debate or logic. For me, I ultimately concluded that the universe, and all its parts and nuances, is simply too complex, and intertwined, to be a random cipher. How complex is it? We live on one planet that is hurtling through space at an enormous speed. At the same time our planet is revolving around its sun, and also spinning on its axis. Out little planet of Earth is located in one galaxy (the Milky Way) which is composed of two hundred billion suns, plus all the attendant planets, moons, and other celestial bodies that are in constant motion. And our one galaxy is just one of two trillion other galaxies that are in the "known" universe. These galaxies are separated from each other with almost unimaginable space ("aether" as the Greeks called it). For me, it is apparent that a greater force (for lack of a better term we can call this force "God") has set the universe in motion and continues to play a significant role in keeping "nothingness" at bay.

So, I believe in God. Does that mean I am a religious man? Probably not, in the traditional sense of the definition of religion.

The diversity of religions is an enigma to me. Christians, Moslems, Hindus, Buddhists, Jews, and many others, plus the divisions and sects within each religion. They can't all be correct.

In my view, the books of religion – all of them – are written by men, and as such, are not divine. The writer may very well believe that the words in the book are "the words of God". But, to me, they are just the words of a man who thinks he has heard the words of God. These books may very well convey important truths that help men and women live better lives. But I do not treat them as any more than the words of men.

And so, I have concluded that I am a Deist. Deism is pretty simple, and that suits me just fine. It is the belief in the existence of a Supreme Being. But, at the same time, a Deist rejects the teachings and trappings of religion as merely the work of men. Interestingly enough, Deism was quite popular during the Age of Enlightenment and included such American luminaries as Benjamin Franklin, Thomas Jefferson, Ethan Allen and Thomas Paine.

At bottom, I believe in a Supreme Being. I am comfortable using the term "God" as shorthand for the Supreme Being. I find it somewhat amusing to see artist's conceptions of God, and author's descriptions of God. In my opinion, mortal beings have about as much insight and understanding of God as an ant does of a human. To me, God is a constant force that has set the universe (with its trillions of galaxies, each with billions of suns and planets, infinite spaces of the known universe filled with things and nothings) in constant motion. That universe is far too complex, yet so finely attuned, that it cannot be merely a random hiccup in time.

And all those religious books and works, and all the musings of saints and seers – they are not the words of God. They are the words of men and women, albeit inspired by thoughts of God. Anyone can "create" a religion – even Joseph Smith or L. Ron Hubbard – if they are clever enough or inspired enough.

So, as a Deist, I have chosen to live a moral life. I suppose a Deist could choose to live an amoral life. Particularly if one doesn't believe in heaven or hell, or any kind of afterlife, I imagine a person could decide that they may as well live a life of fun, lechery and debauchery. But I prefer the moral life. There are three reasons for this. First, it is just easier that way. I think a life of fun, lechery and debauchery would be very labor-intensive, could very well harm one's health, and would ultimately be boring. Second, a moral life is much more orderly and organized. And being an organized and orderly person, such a life is preferred. It has no loose edges and it is not messy. Third, there is God. To be clear: I don't view God as a gray-haired, white-robed gentleman surrounded by cherubs and lightning bolts, nor even as an entity in human form. But, to me, there is a certain level of comfort knowing that God exists. What an empty universe it would be without God! So, there are times I will have a conversation with God. It's a rather one-way conversation, of course. But God is a very good listener, and I can't think of even one time that God has interrupted me. Sometimes I will talk with God out loud, using my voice to say words to the Deity. But most of the time when I talk to God it is silently, with my thoughts. I don't have these talks with God very often, perhaps only once or twice a year, if that. But it is comforting to me to know that I can do that. And when the universe seems set against me, I know I can reach out and articulate my issues.

More often, I just thank God. This usually happens on a very good day, when the sun is shining on the trees and grass, or the moon is bright illuminating the darkness. When I see a blue sky with thick white clouds, and I feel a light breeze on my face. Or it may be a tree or a field of sunflowers. In those moments I will just say, "Thank you, God, for giving me this life. Thank you for these wonderful things." It makes me feel good to be able to thank God like this from time to time, when the spirit moves me. And does God hear me?

Why, of course.

Thirty-Two

Where Do We Go From Here

Many people aspire to write a book, but few actually accomplish the mission. The worst mistake a budding author can make is to write the title of his/her book before he/she actually writes it. Far better to write the book, then the title. The title will be apparent once the book is written – and this is particularly true with an autobiography.

I enjoyed writing a science fiction novel in 1986. Science fiction is great fun. The slate is completely blank and in science fiction, anything goes and anything is possible. An autobiography is the exact opposite. The book has already been written – it just has to be told. And so as I put the finishing touches on my autobiography, the title of the work came into focus. Those who know me well probably remember my favorite expression: "I spit on retirement." I have said it often, particularly in the last few years as I entered (and passed) the normal "retirement age". We all go through stages in our lives: high school, college, first job, weddings, births, new jobs, promotions, honors, retirements, deaths. Retirement is kind of an accepted stage of life. Most people I know really look forward to that last day on the job. I know people who count the years, months, even days till that final day when they can hang it up and do all the things that they have wanted to do all the working days of their lives.

Many of my friends have recently retired. In fact, the circle of my friends who are still working is an ever-diminishing circle. They universally express delight with being retired.

But, not me. Bottom line – I love to work, and I have loved the work I have done in my life. I don't golf, or garden, or collect things, or play cards. I even disconnected the television sets in my home because I find television mildly amusing but mainly an exercise in mental masturbation. It's just not a productive use of my time. On the other hand, my work gives me not only great pleasure, but I feel that I have made and continue to make a contribution. My life, ever since I was 17 till the present has been focused on and dedicated to service. I believe my time on earth has improved the human condition of people around me. To me, that is very satisfying.

So, now that I am in my 70's and folks invariably ask me when I'm going to retire, I say, "I spit on retirement." I don't mean to denigrate anyone else's plans for retirement nor the institution of retirement. I respect it. In fact, for years I served as a member of the Board of Directors, and as Chairman of the Odd Fellows Homes of California, which has oversight of two wonderful retirement campuses in Saratoga and in Napa. Retirement is fine – for those who long to do it. It's not for me.

Oh sure, I receive social security retirement income because it is accrued and I have to take it. And I receive retirement income from the Public Employee's Retirement System because I put in over 20 years of service in public employment. But I'm still working full time as a Judge. I'm now in the Judicial Retirement System and in 2020 I will have 17 years in that system. I could have retired from JRS years ago, and in 2023 I will hit 20 years in the JRS system and will have "maxed out" my retirement benefits. At that point I could stop working as a Judge and receive 75% of my pay – for the rest of my life. In other words, if I keep working past 2023, I will be working for 25% of my Judge's pay. But, honestly, I've never been in it for the money. Why have I been "in it"? For the job satisfaction, for dedication to public service, and because I really like to work. I also have all this life experience and experience as a Judge that would essentially evaporate if I were to retire. At bottom, I think the defendants who appear before me, the victims, the attorneys, the members of the public who serve as jurors – all appreciate being in the courtroom with a Judge who has a lifetime of experience and a few gray hairs.

I may be part of a small phenomenon in 21st century America. Used to be that when one turned 65, one was expected to retire and sit on the porch rocking chair. Today, more and more men and women in their 70's continue to remain in the work force. There are many reasons for that, primarily economic – they need the money. That's not my reason. I don't need the money. What I need is the work. I suspect I would be bored otherwise.

So, where do we go from here? Well, that's a darn good question. As I write these memoirs I approach the age of 75. So long as my health allows and my memory doesn't fail me, I see no reason to pasture myself. Perhaps I will write a sequel to this autobiography when I turn 85 . . .

Do autobiographies ever have sequels?

Lea and Dave in 2020

Does this man look like he is ready to retire?

Acknowledgments

A special thank you to Aaron Wedra, owner of Smartz Graphics in Davis California and fellow member of the Davis Odd Fellows Lodge #169, for laying out my autobiography in Adobe InDesign.